HERMIT CRAB

Illustrated 2nd Edition

Sail A'non

Copyright © 2017 Ömer Akın
All rights reserved
ISBN: 0-9762941-5-X

*Dedicated to Canan, Azra, and Kaan
and the Loving Memory of*
Dr Mete Akın

HERMIT CRAB - Sail A'non

Credits
Cover Design by Ayça Akın
Illustrations by Ömer Akın

Disclaimer
All characters depicted in this novel are fictional except when they are not, and you'll know it.

Contents

	Preface
Chapter 1	*Disquiet*
Chapter 2	*Resolve*
Chapter 3	*Bedlam*
Chapter 4	*Persistence*
Chapter 5	*Toil*
Chapter 6	*Aplomb*
Chapter 7	*Nouement*
Chapter 8	*Deouement*
Chapter 9	*Goad*
Chapter 10	*Exodus*
Chapter 11	*Bliss*
Chapter 12	*Breakdown*
Chapter 13	*Tumult*
Chapter 14	*Redemption*

HERMIT CRAB - Sail A'non

Preface

Some things are best kept to yourself. Malicious intent, bigotry, in-laws, heartaches, or even hemorrhoids can find a sympathetic ear. My problem however is unique in this respect. If I reveal it to a single soul, it will instantly become a deeper and more intractable one.

I want to change. That is not as the result of a new year's resolution or some midlife crisis; but in a more fundamental way. I want to cease being one thing and become something else, instantly and indubitably. My father would call this a tsuris shmeer; and then he would conclude with a vaguely audible oy vey*!*

I am in my early fifties. Have a wife, a son, a house, and a job – well, sort of a parade of jobs that have left me wondering what I want to do in life. What I'm sure of is I want to stop being Edward – that's me. I want a complete change. It's as simple as that. I want a steady job, a small house, new clothes, new appliances, a new family: a new life that is complete with all of its various *accoutrement*.

Under normal circumstances, I could get divorced abandon my life as I know it and move on to doing all of those things. But I do not have the chutzpah to go through with it. I suppose you guessed by now that I am Jewish. My wife, Kay is Catholic, which sets up the double indemnity for my dilemma. Even if I somehow got her to agree to a divorce, which is not a supposition I could make with the slightest amount of confidence, cannons of both of our religious institutions would catapult our family clans into unimaginable bouts of outrage. I cannot even get myself to solemnly consider the mashooginah that would result from bringing the subject up with anyone.

To make matters worse, I am a certified wimp. This character flaw, which I've had for as long as I can remember, is also recognized by most of my family members; thanks to my father, who never missed an opportunity to call me a *schnook*. One of the earliest recollections I have of my father's famous insults added to injury is the "snake in the grass" incident, at my Aunt Esther's backyard. I was around six and vaguely familiar with the real meaning of this phrase. It happened when I was playing hide-and-go-seek with cousins and family friends.

At that time, my panache for research had convinced me that grass would conceal all slithering reptilian creatures until it was too late. Not having seen a snake in real life I could only imagine from pictures that carelessness would inevitably lead to a painful bite and distribution of agonizing poison in your veins ultimately leading to the termination of promising life; my life.

Since the days when I had realized these morbid aspects of life particularly on suburban lawns that were not well maintained, I had developed this unhealthy curiosity about snake pictures wherever I could find them. I kept imagining the torturous deaths they would cause their victims: postulant rancid bite wounds, brown froth oozing from all orifices of the face, and excruciating pain in the heart, where I always imagined, as a child, the source of one's life resided. This was truly an acute childhood psychosis.

Once I was paralyzed before a billboard depicting a coiled king cobra exposing two huge fangs, as my mom tried in vain to pry me loose from the sidewalk onto which my feet were glued stuck, all the while when my dad was moving on, shaking his head, and mumbling his favorite lament: oy vey!

On one fateful summer day in Aunt Esther's backyard, spotting, ever so briefly, the slithering brown creature shimmering in the sunlight concealed under an overgrown grassy patch was enough to have my well-honed imagination confirm imminent danger. I ran inside with considerable panic, crying "snake in the grass!" as loud as I could. I was intent on saving everyone. All male adults, except uncle Joe, who complained endlessly about his gout, especially when physical exertion of any kind presented itself, marched on out to the spot that I gingerly approached in the safety of the human shield my adult relatives created. As soon as I saw a small glimmer of the slithering creature, I pointed and yelled: "There it is!" This was enough to bring the posse to a dead stop.

Much to my chagrin, upon closer examination, my dangerous foe, presenting a threat to my entire family, turned out to be an unusually elongated fecal phenomena deposited by Daisy, the family Great Dane, ailing from a type of canine diarrhea. My father had no hesitation to ridicule me on the spot and send me to my mom with the question: "to whom did I owe my superior genes?" He telegraphed this query at the top of his lungs to mom who was cowering behind the screen door of the kitchen.

My dad was a WWII vet in desperate search of evidence of *D-day* chutzpah in his only child. To make matters worse, as my dad offered the speculation that I possessed a deep rooted *fear-of-turd*, it was Margaret my five year old cousin, who was the first one to reveal my erring ways. Dad explained that I must have inherited this condition from mom's side of the family. To this day, during each family gathering, there still is some joker who will remind me of this unfortunate attribution.

I always had the feeling that, despite the overt display of disdain, my father loved me deep down inside. When it comes to Jay, my son, I do not pepper indifference with chaffing remarks, in order to hint at my affection. He is the only thing in my life that I truly enjoy.

He is smart and full of potential. He has almost his entire life ahead of him. He is only twelve and-a-half years old. He is curious and an avid reader. He's a bit of an introvert, but not bashful or timid like me. He has friends and does very well in school. He looks nothing like me but neither did I when I was his age. I hope he will achieve the happiness for which I am still longing. I cannot wait to see what kind of person he will become. However, if my plan works, I will not be around to see it.

This would be one of my greatest regrets, trumped only by my insatiable desire construct a new life for myself. The only reason I did not put my plan into action until now has been on account of my affection for Jay.

HERMIT CRAB - Sail A'non

HERMIT CRAB - Sail A'non

One
Disquiet

Did I say I am 53 years old? I feel forgetful sometimes. Based on my ancestry, my life expectancy affords me, at best, another 25 years. I have already squandered two-thirds of my life in my present miserable state. When I start anew, I will have to allow sufficient time for my new life to take root, branch out, and flourish so that I would have some quality time left to enjoy. I have no time to spare since I have been longing for self-fulfillment for far too long.

"What?"

Kay's voice both startled and agitated me. Waking from my inner thoughts of malicious mischief was like being caught with both hands in the cookie jar. I feel guilty even thinking about my intentions.

"Yes honeybunch! I'll clear the dining table, just as soon as I get down."

...

"Huh? You know I need to complete that report for tomorrow. Can't we just eat at the kitchen table?""

...

"What? Jay's friend is coming to dinner?"

...

"Who? I did not know he had close friends. OK, OK, I'm on my way."

Shuffling down the stairs, I revealed my discontent in a voice loud enough to satisfy my ego but not so she could hear me.

"I'll take care of it right away. You know if I had a study of my own I would not have to clutter the dining table with all this stuff."

My wife occupies our only spare bedroom with her projects. I end up being the nomad working at the dining table, the low bedroom credenza, or anywhere else where I can find uncluttered horizontal space to lay out my books and files. As inconvenient as this is, there is a morsel of satisfaction in it for me as well. It drives Kay nuts to find my clutter all over the place.

To digress, the only reason we were able to afford this house was because my parents practically gave a starter-house to us as a wedding gift. And we bought this one after making a sizeable profit by selling the starter-house. So if anyone has more right to the use of the space we have now, it should be me. My inheritance got us in here!

Yet, to be fair, if it weren't for Kay's steady and relatively well paying job we would have had a hard time making payments. Under an ordinary portioning of equity, I would not fuss over such anal calculations about real estate.

On the other hand, Kay has anything but an ordinary sense of fairness. She acts as if she is entitled to the entire bowl of wax. Take for instance the library I used to have in our starter-house which all but disappeared during the transition to this house. It was not much in terms of quality of space. It was tucked into the basement yet it meant everything to me. It was my haven, my escape, my identity, my sanity.

I was just a freshman at college when I started my book collection. Every day, when I came home from school – this was way before I was married = I would go straight to the basement. I would inspect the shelves full of carefully ordered morsels of intellect, like so many layers of armor against ignorance. Over the years, I amassed an impressive collection of political science and history books. If only I had been able to keep my library intact during our move to our current house, by now, it would have been the envy of most erudite souls.

The narrow stairway and the rickety door at the head of the basement stairs, which was difficult to close since it scraped with a loud squeak against the bent aluminum threshold, served as my drawbridge against the world. While the scratching of the threshold announced anyone approaching, I could not sneak in or out with ease either.

My books were neatly stacked on wooden shelves lined against the walls. The shelves were functional but old and irregularly sized. They were stained pine construction; not your ordinary plastic-veneer particleboard that you can pick up at IKEA or any secondhand place like the local Goodwill. They had an indigenous patina with a rugged look of age, something I considered impressive as a youngster.

Even in the dark and damp air of the basement, which did not help my asthmatic constitution one bit, you could detect the nuts and grains of the B-grade solid wood under its dark walnut stain. In the summer when the moisture was high, you could smell the pine. Wood species are able to carry their inner nature decades after they have been cut down, milled, dried, and stained with chemicals: a feat any human would envy. Once we are embalmed, our only hope is to rot with some dignity and minimum effervescence.

The fluctuating humidity of the basement, not to mention the weight of the books, had contributed to the sagging of the shelves, with a rhythm punctuated by the staccato of the shelving uprights. The entire thing had a pleasant touch of pathos. The books complemented this through an inherent sense of pride. They were lined up in rows with care according to subject matter and size.

While they had different thicknesses and colors I did not have to forego the Dewy Decimal System. In this way I could keep all books in a certain subject and with a certain height on the same shelf. I did not have to sacrifice shelf height just because one book, say 24 inches high, had to be on a shelf with 10 inch-high books; a problem of shelf-aesthetics I had observed in the library of an acquaintance, about whom I will tell you momentarily.

Annone, a second generation Italian-American, and Kay's co-worker, has a real eclectic taste for books. In a given set of books on a subject, he will buy the most affordable ones that pass his minimum standards of quality, which are farshlugginer. (Lamentably, I think I am turning into my father.)

Annone's library contains random collections of publishers, formats, genres, of which there are many. He ends up with tall art catalogs purchased at the National Gallery of Art side by side with pocket size books by Gombrich and Grabar. His library furnished with proverbial IKEA shelves and irregular book heights on each shelf creates an almost Post-Modern appearance that I dislike nearly as much as the *ad hoc* nature of his collection.

My basement library, modest in its cost and appearance, looked more like an intentional design stylized after the garlands of Rococo or floral transoms of Art Nouveau owing largely to the bowing of the horizontals under the weight of the books, moisture in the air, and uniformity of size. Beauty is, after all, held in the eyes of the beholder.

"When are we going to get rid of these books?"

Kay's voice echoed from the past, reaching the deep crevices of my brain still preoccupied with the cozy basement of our first house. It also brought back memories of the same exchange I heard so many times when we were happy, at least content, newlyweds in that matchbox of a house.

"Didn't we agree that we would?"

At this moment, I am no longer sure, if I am, let alone if my thoughts are, at the current house or the former. The refrain is at once an echo in my brain and a sound wave reaching my ears, surreally transcending time.

"You know we cannot move to the new house with all of this junk. These books are calcified."

Confirmation: my mind is at the former house!

"Besides all the mildew and book mites will have you heaving and snorting like Felix Unger all night long. If I'm going to continue to be the sole breadwinner I need to get my sleep. Besides, if we don't get it to look at least 'normal.' we will not be able to sell the house for the asking price. This basement looks like a medieval dungeon!"

During all the years we've been married she does not realize that I consider this kind of attribution a perfect compliment. I still visualize the library at the abbey in the *Name of the Rose,* whenever I have comforting daydreams about libraries.

"I bet most of these books are glued shut with years of moisture and mold."

...

"What? No, we will not move them to our new house! I won't stand for it."

...

"That'll fuckup the new house before we even set foot in it."

This is when I hate her most, a shrill, finger-shaking shiksa. I am not a bigot but there are times when I revert to my father's lingo if not state of mind. Chalk it up to nurture, not nature.

"Do you realize how many boxes it will take to pack up this crap? And these shelves... ...we should donate them to a landfill!"

"What? The movers? They will have a field day with this that is if we can afford movers. If the place is going to be run over by these gaggles of

Guttenberg-gooks, I am not paying a dime of my hard earned money to move them."

This was Kay's way of blending sarcasm with wit in her own pathetic way, even though I must admit I was impressed with her effort to integrate historical highlight into her daily dose of drek – ha, ha; two can play at this.

Dismantling of my library, which looked inevitable each passing day, will literally break the last strand that connects me to Kay and my identity as Edward for some 40 years. This will mark the beginning of the end of my current life.

My resolve to abandon that identity and life was set when Kay invited Annone and his neighbor George to pick out a *few* of my books, in order to lighten our load during the *big* move to the *new* house. Of course this was arranged ahead of time and without my knowledge or consent, another illustration of Kay's idea for *compromise* and *consent* between the two of us. She always assumed that I consented to the compromises that she sketched out all by herself.

I knew what to expect from Annone. He is an eclectic, a scavenger looking for a good deal with little regard for merit in his overall collection. He will be satisfied with a few books he considers good enough, whereas I am a true collector. I work meticulously for the love of my intellectual pursuits in Western Philosophy, History and Political Science.

While at first glance these are different disciplines, they are interconnected through lineage, scholarship and personalities that constitute the veins and arteries running through them to nourish my mind as in a well-tuned biological organism. I feel I know each of my books personally. I recall when and how I acquired them in addition to where and why they belong in my web of intellectual intercourse. I read almost all of them. I am the genuine article.

What about George? I had no idea what to expect before I made his acquaintance; that is if making acquaintance is like stepping on a wasp's nest. I had no inkling that, one fateful evening, I would meet the *Dungeon Master,* the *Thor* of book augers. I was not prepared for this; not at all.

So let me digress. George, like Annone, turns out to be a scavenger; yet he is also a deep feeder with a much larger scope. He buys entire holdings or closeout collections from churches, libraries, schools, and book stores. In addition to the 20,000 volumes of regular stuff, he has first editions, limited editions, and rare books. He acquires from fellow collectors in lump, either when they get in trouble with spouses, get divorced, get too old or kick the bucket. He does this at such a compulsive pace that according to Annone he has a "serious addiction problem," which is also manifest through his gambling compulsion.

The two neighbors often hunt together. They have a parasitic relationship. Annone is George's cover for his wife and George is the explorer that finds the "gold mines." On Saturday evenings, George buys the local Sunday paper and scans the ads for book sales - he is still not up on web technology. Then he calls the most promising ones, before all the ordinary buzzards descend upon the sale, to arrange a sneak preview session with the promise of lump sum purchases.

Years after they ravaged my library, Annone told me about one of George's more memorable book buying binges. In this garage sale, there was a lot of men's stuff on sale: shoes, pants, shirts, ties, belts, suites, jackets, tools, referee uniforms, soccer balls, and of course books. Annone and George moved in right to the book section and discovered a sizeable architectural collection which turned George's overdrive on since he is an architect. By the time Annone, who was an architect as well, discovered the book collection, it was too late. This was the real gold mine he was hoping to find for a long time.

This is when Annone first saw his buddy's addiction in its stark naked form. George was hunched over the table of books – he is 6'-2" tall often wearing baggy pants and a t-shirt acquired from the local Goodwill – and mumbling to himself. He would look at a book for about a second or two scanning the title, author, publisher, inside cover and the wear on the binding like an automaton and make his decision instantly. Any seconds lost would mean the potential loss of a book still waiting to be processed. He would quickly put the selected book on a pile on the ground, which grew taller at an alarming rate, and then move on to the next one. When that pile of books grew tall enough, he would sit on it either to keep it from tipping over or discourage any potential pickpockets, and continue his selections from a more comfortable and secure posture.

"Oh boy! Oh boy!"

This utterance, coming out of the mouth of this talk, lanky, erudite, architect dressed like a bum sitting on a pile of books and grabbing more with the intensity of an industrial machine, was both amusing and disturbing -- as I too would attest to, one fateful day, based on what I witnessed in my own house.

"Why would anyone sell these for a buck? Oh boy! Oh boy!"

Intense pleasure and excitement making a grown man hyperventilate is a rare sight. On the way out of the garage sale, Annone recognized the woman selling all of this stuff for next to nothing. She was a fellow soccer referee. The brief greeting turned into a chat about her husband, another fellow referee. Recently, she had discovered that he was screwing around. She kicked him out of the house with scarcely more than a tooth brush. The garage sale was part of the process of purging him from her life. All of the "grime that the leech left behind" had to be cleansed thoroughly until not even a little speck was left. As the saying goes, someone's trash is someone else's treasure.

While I have been planning my less than graceful exit from Kay's life, a persistent source of discouragement has been the images of my books, in due time, being, sold, given away, and tossed into garbage with contempt and impunity. These disturbing impressions are all that I took away from Annone's vivid anecdote. I always considered Kay's giveaway of my books to these two opportunists, George and Annone, a dress rehearsal of the inevitable "final solution" of my library. Mercifully this eventuality belongs to a future that will not include me as a tortured witness. Oy vey!

When George and Annone arrived at my house, "to pick out a few books," I was in the bathroom. I had been nervous since the moment Kay called me at work and told me that they were coming that evening. I had to takeoff early from work to organize number of books on tables as my sacrificial set, offered up, in a valiant attempt to keep the rest of my collection intact.

During those days, Kay's cooking did not agree with my delicate digestive constitution either, and my hemorrhoids were aflame. It was either the food or the anxiety of the buzzards encircling my library that caused a disconcerting inflammation. I tried desperately to empty my bowels. Rushing and pushing are the kiss of death for those tits of the anal realm. I could overhear the small talk Kay was making with Annone and George at the door. It was brief. "Push, push" god damn, it hurts.

I was desperate to go out there and witness the imminent massacre being staged in my lair of literary lexicon. Taking a deep interest in witnessing that which is painful is one of man's poorly understood psychological weaknesses. Why, for instance, are people, wrapped in a fireman's blanket, unable to take their eyes off of their burning house, as every little bit that vanishes before their eyes is a stab of pain in their heart?

Motivated by a similar instinct, I moved out of the bathroom like a zombie in a trance. I could hear the squeak of the basement door. The drawbridge is breached. I gathered myself as quickly as possible and shuffled away from the bathroom and down the steps, in that trademark motion that hemorrhoid sufferers know all too well and try to conceal. This is a stride that is a mix between John Wayne's machismo pace and Madame Butterfly's delicate glide; that is, if anyone can truly imagine such an amalgam.

By the time I made my way to the basement, the attack was well underway. I descended the steps slowly like a commander carrying out orders against his better judgment. The look of pain in my face was mostly due to my anal discomfort but it suited the occasion all too well. Yet, I did not want to appear overly distraught and give aid to the enemy. So I gathered myself up in as nonchalant a gait as this fat, balding, middle aged, bookworm could muster and reached the bottom of the stairs. In another setting, my predicament might have evoked a vivid image of Norma Desmond's final descent. Metaphors were swirling in my brain, helping my alienation from reality that amounted to the destruction of my library.

Annone and George had hardly noticed my presence. They, the enemy, were busy selecting books from the tables in the middle of the room. One was a large work bench, 3' x 8', able to hold more than a hundred books in one layer. I had more than 150 on that one. The small card table of Sears Roebuck Catalogue vintage, with collapsible metal tubular legs, was barely supporting the load of nearly one hundred books piled on it.

I had to create an impression of abundance mostly for Kay's eyes; in order for the *mission* to be satisfactorily completed and for the bleeding to stop, at least for now. If Kay thought that I did not eliminate sufficient number of books, there would be hell to pay; and more, much more of my collection would be sacrificed.

My heart was sinking. With each passing minute a handful of books were being moved from the table to cardboard boxes, conveniently positioned by Kay around the tables. Annone and George seldom uttered a word. With some satisfaction, I realized that the quality of even the discards of my collection had captured their interest sufficiently to distance them from the frantic behaviors that buzzards exhibit as they dismantle a carcass. It was quiet, almost like a viewing.

I remembered Kay's aunt's viewing at her family's favorite funeral home, where I wore my yarmelkeh, almost instinctively and out of respect. She did not miss the opportunity to blame and ridicule me for confusing rituals. My mind was playing sophisticated games of distraction with me.

I came closer to the table to inspect the cadaver. There were plenty of wounds hollowed out of the neatly ordered rows of books. The structure was breached, the castle walls were impaired, and the defenses were about to fall. I could not think of anything appropriate to say. My lips took over.

"So there're some books you would like to have, huh?"

At such an awkward moment, what is more stupid and comforting than stating the obvious? Their response resembled that of an obese man with a mouthful of grub

"Huh, huh."

This was the first time I had seen, can't really say met, George. Not even a greeting was uttered. They were totally oblivious to me.

"Hey dickheads these are my books!" screamed something inside me which mercifully did not reach my lips. I moved a little bit closer. I stood behind Annone. Shirer, Kissinger, Toynbee, Corbin, Lehman … Pain! He's picked some good ones. I walked around to George's pile. Since they were unaware of me or my movements, I was no longer trying to be inconspicuous. George was also picking good ones and at a faster pace. He had two and a half boxes already filled. Methodical, efficient, thorough are the adjectives that come to mind: a real pro!

But wait! No not this one. Did I put this on the table with my own hands? I couldn't have. The first edition of Umberto Eco's *Semiotics*; not a chance! As these thoughts were racing in my head, at the blink of an eye I felt the adrenalin rush and heard a voice from inside, this time going through my lips:

"Wait! I want to keep this one."

It was not a threatening voice but one filled with quiet resolve. This got George's attention. Annone also looked in my direction. George leaned over and picked Eco's *Semiotics* and put it in the box even closer to him.

"I want to keep this one" I repeated.

"I already got it." George said matter-of-factly.

I was puzzled by his nonchalant dismissal of the embarrassing situation. This was no encounter in a sandbox at the playground. This was serious business; yet with childlike innocence I reached out and picked the book up. With uncommon agility and without hesitation George grabbed the other end of the book. This will have to do for the handshake that we never had.

"Your wife said we could pick anything off of this table... I found it right there."

"But I want to keep this one."

I could not say it was not on the table for fear that I might insult him. Besides I was not entirely sure that I did not make the mistake myself.

"But this is a first edition"

I declared, hesitating for an instance in the middle of my sentence fearing that it may make the prize even more attractive; but quickly realized that this is something that would not escape George anyway.

"No, you don't want to keep it. I already got it."

Courtesy and civility were rapidly evaporating. I tried to yank the book out of his hands. His grip was too tight. I felt his reciprocal pull which in turn tightened my hold on Umberto. *Semiotics* was frozen in midair between the two of us. I could feel George's bony knuckles pressing against my fingers. This was the moment of truth. "I will rescue you my Umberto" the inaudible retort spurred me on. "What good is a commander who cannot save even a single soldier?" I yanked harder. The old goat was stronger than I thought.

"But I want to keep this one" while my voice displayed resolve my hands were beginning to shake.

"George, let go!"

We both heard an arbitrator's voice chime in. It was Annone. Having watched this childish display from a distance, for far too long, he had decided to intervene. He was responsible for bringing George over.

"It's his book after all."

This made no noticeable impression on George.

"We are at his house, they invited us!"

Remarkably this seemed to make an impression on George and he suddenly let go. I was not prepared for this. The residual force from my tug was sufficient to cause me to lose my balance. I started falling backward. I tripped on one of those damn boxes and barely noticed that *Semiotics*, first edition, Indiana Press, 1984, flew right out of my hands before I tumbled down and hit the floor with my already bruised ass and the shelving with the back of my head. The next thing I remember is Kay, Annone, and George helping me up the stairs onto the living room sofa. I was as perplexed and dizzied as a stinkbug banging around, inside a lampshade.

Apparently, Annone and George left my house with several boxes full of books. I was too out of it to participate in the awkward goodbyes exchanged with Kay. I vaguely recall overhearing a conversation for the sole purpose of explaining that this was just an innocent accident. Indeed!

My "stolen" books, my head, my hemorrhoids were all killing me. When I woke up the next morning with a headache, one of the first things I did was to inspect the basement. The tables were cleaned out. Kay had packed the leftovers for

Goodwill before she left for work. Eco's *Semiotics* was nowhere to be found.

I felt utterly defeated. The battle is lost, but the war is just beginning. As soon as my head and rear end are sufficiently healed, I will put my plans into action and begin the process of healing my soul. The call to arms is sounded against the true enemy: Kay!

HERMIT CRAB - Sail A'non

HERMIT CRAB - Sail A'non

Two
Resolve

Most people would be content with being in my shoes. The trouble is I will be far more content in someone else's. You may think that my exasperation is at best juvenile; and I should just suck it up and deal with it; yet, juvenile or not, it is personal! I have to see it through.

Kay's book-giveaway was the last straw that shattered my endurance for domestic life. My entire existence, up to this point in time, has been shored up by the emotional braces I bring along from the solitary days spent with my books in that ramshackle basement library I built one book at a time. However indications are that the foreseeable future will be full of indignities of the kind I suffered in George and Annone's hands. Things have gotten so bad that, several times a day, I cringe just thinking about these highlights of humiliation, daily berating and ridicule I suffer in Kay's hands.

What are my options? Honestly. I have very few. If I so much as broach the subject of divorce, I would never survive the resulting catharsis. Aside from the religious cannons we have to work around, the families would go nuts and Kay simply amok. This option is out of the question. It would still end up with the status quo and furthermore my stock would diminish a few more notches in everyone's esteem, including mine.

I am not close minded. I would consider other options including: murder, suicide, or both. Desperate times require desperate measures. But these involve violence – something I could neither morally condone nor be able to undertake. Remember, I am a certified woos. Besides it would be devastating for Jay.

However, if any of these more dramatic options would come to pass quite by themselves, I could compromise my ethics a bit and quietly rejoice. Whereas doing an overt act of violence to a human being, including me is unthinkable. Sneaking, lying, and cheating are covert acts that suit my character much better. Once I disappear, I would not have to face any of the falling out. I am a coward and knowing this does not bother me one bit.

Let us review the facts once again. I was born to Morton and Judith Amado, almost exactly 53.5 years ago, in Baltimore, Maryland, USA. I have a wife, Kay, and a son, Jay. We live in the suburbs of

Baltimore-DC area, 714 Gist Ave, Silver Spring, to be exact. As I told you before, this is the second house Kay and I purchased, this time without help from my parents. I succeeded to rescue only a small portion of my library during the move. Kay kept her entire baking, embroidery and jamming supplies and paraphernalia, outdoing my payload of books by at least a 50%.

Once again, the spare bedroom became hostage to Kay's hobbies, leaving the bits and pieces of vacant real estate around the house as my nomadic work space. The dining room is the largest room of the house. But since we now have Jake the Conure located prominently in a corner of the dining room, this rules out any possibility of me squatting there.

Since Jay and I are mildly asthmatic and cannot coexist with dog or cat dander, Kay acquired Jake as another one of her compromise solutions. It turns out that Jake the Conure is not the best ally to our respiratory problems. With mechanical regularity, it grooms itself several times a day flaking away tiny bits of feather into the air. I think the son of a bitch simply hates me.

Jake is an intelligent bird with a domineering personality. When I get close to his cage he makes this characteristic hissing and clacking sound. When I'm at a distance, he usually bobs around flailing his wings and singing a joyful cadence of staccato yelps. These days, I call it *Jake's Hide*.

Once, when Kay had delegated me to the task of feeding him, it bit me with a vengeance, and nearly took off a piece of my thumb. First it dug its sharp arched upper beak into my flesh, then paused for a moment, looked right at me with his left eye, and then released my thumb – for an instant, reminding me of my Umberto episode with George. It was like a warning shot across the bow.

These days, Kay functions as an assistant to her boss, Mr. Ostergaard. By the same token she hardly ever brings work home; however, when she does, watch out. You would think it is the planning of the Mission to Mars. Her "projects" also include extracurricular tasks like jamming, baking, and embroidery. The number of magazines, jars, boxes of fabric, yarn and recipes, not to mention junky literature piled around the spare room is enough to make any grown human being empathize with victims of obsessive compulsive disorders. When I think that this is the tradeoff for the space I need for my research, writing, and books, I can scream, silently of course.

Our living room is very small, and it lacks character. It is where Kay entertains guests from work several times a year. My parents and in-laws visit us on alternate Saturday's when we are not visiting them. We often spend our time in the dining room which seats twelve around a large table that leaves just enough room for Jake's cage and Kay's china cabinet. Outwardly she takes great pride in her crystals collection. I suspect this is her way of countering my passion for collecting books. I loathe her vanity as well as her rag tag assembly of glass trinkets.

When I first met Kay, I was working part-time for a headhunting agency in Baltimore. Mr. Ostergaard, my parent's neighbor, who was the owner and CEO of the Ad-Ventures Placement Agency Inc., relenting to my parent's constant prodding, hired me. By quitting my job at the Greater Baltimore Sanitation Department and reaching the big 4-0, inadvertently, I had made my mother extremely nervous. She was sure that I was on my way to becoming a permanent mama's boy: a looser, living-with-parents-way-past-his-prime. For me, however, it was just a stage. I merely lacked a life companion, a job that would fulfill my true potential, and enough time for reading and writing. To make matters worse, I neither had the physical dexterity nor the coordination to fall back on mastering a musical instrument or excelling in sports, which would have helped dispel the lazy bum image that I depicted so convincingly during large family gatherings.

My dad wanted me to become a lawyer or doctor, but I could not stand the sight of blood, even if it were mine; and lawyers struck me as somewhat disingenuous. All of those whom I met during family gatherings had airs about them that made me suspicious about their true qualifications. History, a subject I loved since childhood was another guide. As much as I admired Cicero's intellectual pursuits and legislative skills, his ethics did not impress me. It may strike you as strange that I would make career choices based on historical figures, but I have been unusual in my reasoning since childhood – perhaps unusual is somewhat mild; strange would be a better description. Yet, as a child I was entirely comfortable with myself. These days, I desperately long for that feeling.

Ad-Ventures Agency (AVA) Inc. where I found my most stable work opportunity helped me overcome this state of uncertainty in my life. Not only did I find some professional fulfillment in my new position; I also found Kay. When we first met at AVA Inc., I believed her to be attractive and charming. During the years when I was still a bachelor and green behind the ears, a series of serendipitous events at AVA changed my fortunes.

Mr. Ostergaard asked me to find candidates to head our own temp division, the principal responsibility of which was to service the Human Resources Office of the University of Maryland. There had been a good deal of turnover in this position and Mr. Ostergaard was keen on getting it right this time. Previous appointees were not only challenged by stated or unstated qualifications, such as the tenacity to deal with temps, they also lacked the chutzpah to stick with a job that lacked social merit.

Temps usually had equal doses of insecurity and incompetence, while being unaware of either or both. Hence the person to manage of them, whom I was supposed to find, had to deal with dissatisfied clients at various departments of the university not to mention pissed-off temps, believing that they got the short end of the stick for one reason or other. As you try your best to appease department heads who hire temps, you need to sift through the real duds to find true talent and a way to keep them employed. In other words, my task was to lineup for Mr. Ostergaard to interview, good salesman with cold hearts and cunning tongues.

The week had started by making calls and identifying from our own employee files potential candidates. It was Friday and I was still unsure of any prospects. When Mr. Ostergaard approached me, I was frantically rehearsing a good explanation for my lack of progress. He took me by surprise and suggested that I join him along with a few others to go out to the Sharp Edge, our favorite watering hole, a blue collar bar with an impressive Belgian beer selection. .

After the AVA bunch sat down around a large round table at Sharp Edge, Dan – this social occasion apparently called for addressing him by his first name – treated us to the first round of pint tall glasses of beer. Later we learned that he was taking advantage of the fact that his wife was out of town.

He was in a jovial mood, which relaxed us all. As the most junior employee of the firm, I was already feeling flattered to be included, even though I realized that this was probably on account of his friendship with my parents. I am sure I was there also to help with the gender balance of the group. AVA is a small firm with about a dozen fulltime employees, most of whom are women with clerical positions.

We were seated at one of the large round tables at a corner of the dining room. I had ordered a Stella Artois that suited my taste very well and did not cause any bloating in the gastro area. As we had finished our first round and I was getting ready to splurge for my second round, a young lady approached our table and inquired about the vacant seats. Since the time we arrived, the bar had become quite crowded. Dan, taking command of the situation and realizing that there were scarcely any free tables left, invited the group to join us.

"We'd love to join you if only you let us buy you the first round." A female voice intoned from behind me.

"I'm afraid that will not be possible, I already beat you to it." Dan replied. "But you are certainly welcome to buy the second round."

This was more than welcoming for this kind of occasion.

"By all means," the voice continued, which made me turn around and look. This was the very first time I laid eyes on Kay.

She continued: "We promise to be good company and will promptly forget all of you once the night is over."

Her good humor pleased everyone and we shifted around the table to make room for the three newcomers, Kay, Lee and Karen. It turned out that they were celebrating Karen's engagement to Bruce, who was out of town.

They were all upbeat and animated before they had even taken a single sip from their mugs. Lee was the agreeable one. She confirmed all that transpired, even endorsing contradictory statements. Karen was perceivably giddy, laughing at every joke and not saying much especially when we quizzed her about Bruce. Kay was clearly the gang leader who stole the show that evening. She jumped in, to complete virtually every sentence Karen started.

"Bruce is a dentist and a nice one at that ..."

"... Except for his Halitosis." Kay added.

Polite laughs around the table signaled companionship rather than hilarity. Enthused, I jumped in.

"Now that you almost have two out of three, aren't you also going to get a dog?"

"What do you mean also; *also* get or *also* dog?

The semantic pun required more mental energy than what a couple of mugs of beer and formal good humor afforded.

"Neither of us is a dog person. We need a large yard if we ever decide to get one. But with both of us working, it's hard to raise a dog."

"I'll take care of the dog for a fee" Kay said with a smirk on her face.

Karen replied. "Or you can take my job and I'll take care of the dog since your fee would probably be more than my take home pay."

This one hit the target; and helped bury the last one that had bombed, under the weight of its verbiage. I was beginning to feel the buzz and readily laughed when others did.

"That's fine with me; you know I'm between jobs..."

Kay was less than sophisticated, pleasantly boisterous, and cautiously flirtatious through it all; just the right formulae for this *ad hoc* gathering. The not so concealed hint that she was available was enough for Dan to take note. He got all business-like for a moment. Speaking directly to Kay, the woman between jobs:

"Here's my business card" Then to both of them. Maybe you can take care of the dog on alternating days, after work."

Kay was visibly delighted by the unexpected lead. I was certain that she would be calling. I took closer note of this smart, cheerful, warm, slightly aged, not pretty but attractive enough woman. She was closer to my age than anyone I had befriended with similar qualities. I had a feeling she took note of my note, since from then on I became the focus of her humor. Some of her lead-ons were discretely flattering. This made me sufficiently self-conscious so that my usually stutter-start oratory became noticeably indolent. As if noticing this she made subtle references to me that were easy to engage, since they contained easy hooks for conversation.

Before the night was out, I was yapping with reckless abandon, which was clearly out of character for me. By the time we left I was tipsy and almost smitten with Kay. I remember thinking that this might have been one of the most important evenings of my life. This prophecy turned out to be true for various reasons that run the gamut over the last dozen years of my life.

Kay landed the Coordinator of Temps position at AVA. From the outset, Mr. Ostergaard liked what Kay brought to the table. Today, she is his right hand. Over the years, she diligently maintained her Sharp Edge disposition: mentally sharp, pleasantly edgy, and slightly flirtatious. At first, I was reluctant to make a move with her, because of this last aspect of her personality. But this was the proverbial double edged sword. As unpleasant as it was when directed at Mr. Ostergaard, it was indubitably flattering when it was aimed at me. The fact that I knew from our familial contacts that Dan was happily married for over 30 years eliminated any concerns of rivalry.

On another fateful Friday, I approached her, albeit sheepishly, to suggest that we may want to revisit that first evening when we met to celebrate my position being converted to a fulltime salaried one with fringe benefits. She already knew about my so-called promotion. She agreed with an angelic expression and a hint that she may have had a hand in my rather premature recognition.

At the conclusion of this first date, we both knew that this was the beginning of something for both of us. After a few more dates, the word got out. I was pleasantly surprised at this tacit, if not genuine, acknowledgement we received from peers, even from the big boss. There was something innocent and charming about our fall-romance that turned serious so quickly.

We discovered that we shared more things than expected at first glance. She earned her Master's Degree in Public Policy at U of M that is also my *Alma Matter*. Since then, like I, she had been bouncing from job to job for the past decade. A series of circumstances, like bankruptcy, hostile co-workers or bosses, glass ceilings, chauvinist pigs, low pay and long hours, no fringe benefits, no overtime pay, resulted in her itinerant condition.

Our commiserations were nothing short of satisfying if not therapeutic. We even found serendipity in our religious roots being strangely compatible – Catholic for her and Jewish for me – for the orthodoxy of the liturgies and her and my personal irreverence of this fact. In most matters of modern life, we could not stand our faith from birth and what they demanded of us. Emboldened by the optimism infused by this mutual prospecting, we had become oblivious to the fact that we wiped the slate clean of all of the potentially lethal incompatibilities between us that were yet to be discovered.

Our courtship was short. Kay really got me out of my shell. She was the more aggressive one. She was 38, never married and eager to deploy her broad hips to the use that nature had intended. Her younger sister and brothers were already married or engaged to be married. She even had a 17 month old nephew, a fact that never vacated her lips.

If it weren't for her I would still be a bachelor devoid of feminine contact except of a motherly kind – discounting the World Wrestling Federation style hugs and wet kisses I routinely received from my aunts, who insist on giving you that "you-adorable-you" look even if you were in your geriatric years. This is a period of my life that I still remember fondly. When Dan would hint at amorous goings on between Kay and me in my parents' presence, my mother would glow with delight while my dad did not alter his stoic stance.

In those days, I wondered why Kay settled for me: a balding, fat, uncoordinated, intellectual Jew with lousy social skills. One theory I had was that I was the runner up to Dan. Knowing what I know about her character now, I wouldn't put it past her that she would go for the bigger bowl of wax before settling for the consolation prize. I am more inclined to believe that than being anointed as her or anyone else's top choice.

To this day, I do not know if anything transpired between Dan and Kay. Pursuant to our nuptials, when the façade gradually but surely dropped, I got to know Kay better. I realize that she is indeed capable of anything when it came to realizing her ambitions. Dan's enthusiastic support of our marital union was another source of suspicion I had. Was he trying to seal the door shut to his moment of weakness with Kay? At first, this was just a wild hunch that I regarded with a healthy dose of incredulity. However, as years passed, at first, I grew jealous given that they still worked very closely together; and yet, later, I grew apathetic as my feelings for Kay made a bout face. I still consider this a likely but unprovable theory. Today, I have better things to worry about than Kay's infidelity with a man her father's age.

Kay is tall with lanky limbs, bony cheeks, slightly protruding eyes and teeth. Her rather enormous ears are cleverly concealed, especially during our early dates, under her long, brown, silky hair that is one of the truly gorgeous features she possesses. I was taken by these individual qualities, which spoke volumes to the difficulties yet to be encountered by an analytical mind, such as mine, in synthesizing the synergy between these attributes.

I realized the grotesqueness of the total effect of her features only when I began to observe her more objectively, particularly when she went into one of her tirades chastising and reprimanding me for some inane daily thing. That's when I found the answer to one of my lingering questions: why did she ever settle for me? If she were any more attractive, she, most certainly, would not have.

She has narrow shoulders and enormous hips. During the first few months of our courtship, the grotesqueness of this proportional incongruity eluded me completely due to that fact that we spent most of our time at bars and restaurants talking about world politics rather than bodily proportions,. With a clearer mind, I would have even drawn a connection between politics and proportions, even between world proportions and body politics; yet for the first time in my life, I was in a haze due to feelings for a woman I had never experienced before. I should have known that all that Belgian beer blurring my judgment was depositing alcohol in my brain and fat in her hips. It was neither helping her shoulders nor my acumen.

When I first made love to Kay, I was too nervous to notice anything. Gradually, I relaxed enough to explore her body more closely with my hands, during foreplay and in the afterglow. She has tiny breasts, celluloid legs, bony feet and hands, and a jug of fat for a belly. For a while, we were good in bed. Sex too went by the wayside after she became pregnant with Jay and we never recovered real physical attraction between the two of us.

Jay's was a very difficult pregnancy and birth. For one thing, it slammed the door shut on any future baby making ventures. Kay would not have anything more to do with it. She was not thrilled with taking care of an infant as she was working on her relatively tender yet satisfying career. In a marriage of convenience rather than one of passionate love, where procreation goes, so does sex. With silent lamentations, I observed myself gliding like drop of lubricating oil from the rim of a KY bottle towards a life of scarce physical contact with the opposite sex.

As a couple we convey parity of some sort. I am chubby, awkward, and slow. Kay is lanky, quick, and smooth. When I fail she complements; when she agitates I calm things down. Kay can talk your ears off, even when she loses her audience. I can't even start before their attention wanes. I delight in deep thought while she is fanciful in her thinking. I am altruistic, she is selfish. I am patient she is agile. We make a perfect *odd couple*.

Jay is more like me, but has combined traits for sure. He has lanky limbs and bonny extremities, yet when he walks he slumps just like I do, seemingly absorbed in thought and oblivious to details around him. He is normally calm but quite excitable with confrontation, He is slow in getting started, but when he does, it is impossible to get in a word edgewise. He is a reader of all sorts of things including my books as well as his mom's magazines. I think he is searching for his identity. Times will become hard for him. I can see how he would make the same mistakes that I made. If only I could be around to help him. But my resolve is firm. I have to save myself and take my final chance for happiness before I can lay down a plan for Jay.

HERMIT CRAB - Sail A'non

Three
Bedlam

My plan is deceptively simple and effectively complicated. I will cease to exist as Edward Amado and rematerialize as a new person, severing all ties to my family, relatives, friends, job, home, and what's left of my book collection. I am willing to give up all for a chance at a new start. With my knowledge and wisdom acquired through years of major screw ups, I will give myself the opportunity to make the right decisions.

I am not searching for my identity; I have found it and l like it. Yet, as long as I'm with Kay my identity is bottled up in a cage like that of Jake the Conure; pacing up and down making scary sounds, hissing at people, and once in a blue moon, when the opportunity arises, taking a deep bite into a thumb but not daring to rip the flesh out. I will cease being a bird in a cage and turn into a hermit crab roaming the ocean depths in some other creature's shell.

One day I will go to bed as Edward and wake up as Robert, Chris, Howard or whomever it turns out to be; leave my house, my clothes, glasses, identity documents, and ride out into the sunset.

As simple as I put this in my own words, in reality, I know that my plan is fraught with potential complications. For this to work, nothing, say, Robert possesses or associates with should be connected to Edward. The amount of detail that needs to be considered is staggering. The plan, once hatched, must be executed with the precision of neurosurgery. With Kay's tenacity and the tools of information technology available in our day-and-age, she will seek me and eventually beat me out of my shell, hermit or not.

In spite of this possibility, I savor the chance to embark upon something as basic as changing my identity and the challenges it presents. Even the thought of planning and executing something that requires such accuracy sends shivers up and down my spine. This is the sort of thing I was created for. Even if it fails to get me happiness in the end, I will still be satisfied just to pull of the transformation I contemplate.

I may sound like a person obsessed with change. What is more fundamental for life or the universe as we understand them? An embryo turns into a human being, a seed into a tree, a worm into a moth, an ugly duckling into a swan, an idea into a beautiful painting, an event into a revolution, the big bang into a myriad of celestial systems, and a living thing into a rotten pile of organic matter. Change is a natural part of life.

Persistence is what is unnatural. I consider my desire to change as a *natural* urge of my being. The problem is I am facing an *unnatural* obstacle in Kay, as an embryo without a nurturing placenta, a seed without soil and water, a worm without a cocoon. I am simply trying to realize the promise of my nature and remove these unnatural impediments.

The difficulty is to define the scope of my task precisely, leaving nothing to chance. What will it consist of? If I grow some facial hair or get a new set of glasses and wear a wig, would I be a different person? Someone I used to know may no longer recognize me. They may even say "you have changed." This is a superficial transformation that can be reversed with ease. This is not the change I am seeking.

If on the other hand, I had cancer and was subjected to unspeakable chemical treatments and surgical procedures, this would change my appearance as well as my inner biological constitution. This would be a more organic and irreversible change. Is this the sort of authenticity I am seeking? Even in a state of cancerous morphology, would I not still be Edward? My loved ones, acquaintances, even people I meet for the first time would all know me as Edward. When they ask me a brand new question and get an answer, even if my response would be different from what I would have said as a healthful person, it would still be recognized as Edward's thoughts and not that of someone else. While my biological being would be altered, my inner being would still be the same.

This is not the change I am after, either. I am attempting a higher form of change, in which I would free my *id* and *ego* giving rise to a new human being who did not exist heretofore, one that has been stifled and caged in by circumstance. This is an ambitious goal to say the least. Yet, I am motivated even enthralled by the possibility of being able to realize it.

My qualifications make me perfectly suited to the task. I am smart, meticulous, persistent, research savvy, and most of all sneaky by nature. I must conceal my intentions from everyone or all will be lost. All details must be perfectly laid out. This requires persistence and continuous reviews of potential breakdowns. There must be contingency plans, and failsafe strategies. I must develop alternative paths to my goal and research each one carefully to increase certainty and reduce risk. I need to build a Swiss watch that will produce a hermit crab. Oy! Vey!

Five years ago, soon after we moved to the new house on Gist Avenue, I began to hatch my plan. At first, it consisted of disconnected feelings of emancipation that were completely detached from daily realities. Soon they turned into this mosaic of quasi-realities distinct from my own. I soon realized that I was painting this picture of a life that I longed for but did not possess. Gradually this turned into an obsession intensifying my normal episodes of daydreaming. In turn, my altered psyche began evoking new found aggression in Kay, or so it seemed. The vicious cycle has been created. The more she tried to push me out of these compulsive behaviors, the more I became drawn to them.

From the perspective of my mission, one fortunate aspect of being in the new house is its relative proximity to D.C. where most federal records and demographics are available for public access. I could get a head start on how to steal an identity from these records. Ultimately, I need to find a job that would allow me access to records that are not readily available to the public. For instance, it would be useful to see records of the Social Security Administration, Internal Revenue Service, or the Census Bureau. Locally the department of Motor Vehicles and Recorder of

Vital Statistics could also be useful. Yet, if you are not an employee with clearance to handle records, all of these databanks are nearly impossible to penetrate.

The basic outline of my plan is to first identify an individual who exists on paper but not in real life. In order to rig elections and inflate petition signatures, politicians invent fictitious persona all the time. However, I find their methods unsuitable and crude for my taste. As much as I love Political Science, I am no fan of politicians or dirty politics for that matter. I will find a more sophisticated and clean way of executing this shell game with real people and real records.

Then, I will begin to construct official papers: a birth certificate, a social security number, a driver's license, credit cards, library and Starbucks membership cards. Any offer of membership will not be turned down until a healthy sized wallet would be busting at the seams. For a short period of time I will have to have duplicate documents which are risky but necessary for a clean break. All correspondence shall be directed to a safe, untraceable address. To receive hard copy documents at a vacant property would be ideal. D.C. provides good opportunities for this as well. I will buy new outfits, a hat, glasses, toiletries and a suitcase.

These have to be inconspicuous brands with ordinary appearance. Goodwill is a possibility – if I use Goodwill, however, I just have to make sure I don't run into someone I know, like George. These items have to be kept at an inconspicuous place until the fateful day. Ed's belongings shall be discarded without trace. I can donate them to Goodwill and save on my next tax return. This will be preferable to abandoning them somewhere where they may attract attention.

The key to the entire plan is to locate or invent the new identity. This is not the same as identity theft practiced for Medicaid, bank, and credit card fraud. Those are used towards materialistic ends and work only for limited periods of time. My purposes and terms are entirely different. I have to find a *vacant* shell and make it work for the rest of my life.

To start on all of this, I needed a cover to travel to D.C. in order to poke around and do the groundwork for turning this basic plan into a precise strategy for action. My ultimate goal should be to land a job at the US Census Bureau. I have already stayed with Ad-Ventures Agency for an uncharacteristically long period of time. Previously, I had held part-time jobs as an assistant manager of a supermarket chain, called *Giant*, and as an outside consultant to the Records and Reports

(R&R) Department that was under the legislative branch of the Zoning and Administrative Hearings function of Montgomery County.

The former was to get Kay off my back, that latter was a term position and I had to leave when the workload diminished. I would have liked to keep it and now it would have been instrumental in my research, yet this was not in the cards.

Even though it is a long shot, I decided to stop by and see my old boss at the R&R department just to explore the possibility of another stint at my old position with the zoning division. I left work early one day feigning malaise and fatigue. By now Mr. Ostergaard was used to my whining personality and did not appear to be overly annoyed by it. Kay was still out to lunch with a few members of her staff. My departure was as inconspicuous as it needed to be.

I took the metro up to 100 Maryland Avenue, the new location of the R&R department. It is on the fourth floor of a nondescript modernist building. You enter the building through a five-story high, horizontally striped, matchbox proportioned entry block, propped up by the lower four story wings to either side of it. The windows are cut into it with the regularity of predetermination. The flag post topping the entry block lines up with the center mullions of the windows arranged with deadly repetition, on each of the five floors of the entry block. I wonder if the county's planning office had a hand in its design. I figure that the steps preventing disabled access at the main entrance attested to the fact that no one consulted the zoning and building codes office properly about universal design requirements.

The only thing pleasant about approaching this building is the evergreens that lead you to the front steps. I notice the apprehension and excitement that is swelling inside me. After thinking about it for years, I am finally beginning to act on my intentions.

The elevator took me to the fourth floor lobby that accessed the R&R department. Drab, gray, drywall surfaces punctured by exaggerated door frames, laid out with the same deadly regularity of the outside façade, line the sides of the corridors that extend to the right and left. This is either a poor stab at East European panel architecture or a missed stab at Western Post-Modernism.

As I was taking a turn towards the left hallway, absorbed in these thoughts, I lost my footing completely and landed on my right buttock and right elbow without anything else breaking my fall. Instinctively, I was able prevent my head from bumping on the floor.

This fall was so sudden and unexpected that for a moment I was not even aware of my surroundings. For a split second I returned to the library in my basement with George and Annone's perplexed expressions staring back at me. Once the cobwebs disappeared, I noticed the yellow alert cone that indicated some kind of cleanup activity, accounting for the slippery floor. A few people were leaning over to ask if I needed help. I turned these offers down and propped myself up to a sitting position. Some were still asking if they should call an ambulance. I did not seem to have any pain. If I did not get up, the spectacle would continue beyond my tolerance for public attention. This bothered me more than an injury ever could.

I tried to get up but my right elbow sent an excruciating pain up my arm and I could only manage to stand on my knees. I used my left arm to get up on my feet. Someone noticing my grimace helped prop me up by my right arm, Ouch! I wish people would stop helping.

"Are you ok?"

The voice was familiar. I turned around. It was Saeed Nada, my old boss at the Zoning Office. He must have been returning from lunch when he recognized me while I was lying on the floor.

"What are you do'in here?"

"Oh, I fell. I think there was some gook on the floor."

I had mistaken his question. I realized this later and he did not bother correct me. Also, I was too embarrassed to have been seen like this by Mr. Nada after all these years. I did not work up the courage to segue way into the job pitch I was contemplating. I mumbled something about looking up an old friend; turned down his offer of hospitality to "take a sip of water or some'thin" at his office. Despite his many years in the US as a naturalized citizen, Saeed, had all of the habits and instincts of an Arab.

I excused myself and walked towards the elevator, taking tepid steps and holding my right arm gingerly. He must have stared at me as I walked away. I'd be too embarrassed to come back to him anytime soon, to pursue the job opportunity I had in mind. Great start! This turned out to be a real dead end. I wonder if someone is trying to tell me something. I am too shaken to go back to the metro stop. My arm is hurting badly and I am not even sure if I broke a bone.

So I took a cab. When the driver asked where to, I realized that I will have a lot of explaining to do if I go straight home. I remembered that our family doctor, Mr. Kiss' office is close by. On the way there, I cooked up a story about how I slipped and fell at the office. He ordered X-rays to be taken and bed rest for a few days along with the usual "take a pain reliever and plenty of liquids" regiment. The X-rays were negative for a break but positive for a hairline fracture which means that I will have a recuperation period of several weeks. Since I am right handed, I will not be able to work. Now I can devote all of my time to my project.

Since my fall, I had a couple of painful but quiet days in bed. When she was at work I got a break from Kay's endless yapping about my being clumsy, careless, uncoordinated, but the tirade resumed as soon as she comes home. She went into one of her nonstop staccato deliveries.

"Aren't you being selfish, as usual?"

"What if you broke a bone or died?"

"What would happen to your family?

"Did you stop to think that you have responsibilities?"

"What kind of an example are you setting for Jay?"

And as usual, ending these monologues with a reminder that: "I was lucky to have Mr. Ostergaard as a boss, since he would not fire me due to my absence from work."

Now that's a thought! Thankyou Kay! This is the perfect excuse to weasel my way out of my job and find one at the Census Bureau.

After a few days, I was able to return to work. At the end of the day I walked into Mr. Ostergaard's office and gave my notice. He was visibly surprised since he was prepared to accommodate my injury time. I thanked him profusely and explained that I could not simply take advantage of our family friendship and his generous offer to keep my position for months while I recuperated sufficiently to use my right hand. He seemed to understand, as much as one understands why wheels are attracted to pot holes, and offered to hire me back if I ever wanted to return.

I have the feeling that he is aware of the tension between me and Kay and probably thinks of this as a blessing in disguise. Couples in the workplace are a classic HR problem preventing staff harmony. No one would know this better than him as the CEO of a headhunting firm.

At home, Kay had a conniption, *a la* Bill Cosby's TV wife upon discovering that Bill served chocolate cake to the kids for breakfast. In this light, Kay has much more of a cause to complain. I endured it as passively as I could. My patient and firm handling of the situation was paramount in diffusing it. I did not beg to be left alone, I did not cry – which I have done during a few occasions– I did not protest too hard, and most importantly of all I refused to give in and go back to my job.

I noticed at least once that there was a flash of doubt in her eyes: "What on earth is going on with him? This is different? What is he up to?"

This set the fear of being discovered in my heart. I must be more careful in covering my tracks from here on. She is too smart and relentless to allow anyone to pull the wool over her eyes. She is capable of seeing through just about anything. I must reassure her.

One day when she came back from work she found me sitting on the john, cradling the cast around my right arm and quietly crying. I was shedding genuine tears of pain. This convinced her that I still am the wimp that she knows too well. I had resorted to method acting and slammed my right arm against the bathroom door to induce real pain. It worked. She is affectionate and comforting, which lasted for a day or two. Now I need to go the extra mile to appease her. I must take the first opportunity to find a job.

The following day, I found an online ad for a floor manager's position at the local *Border's* that is walking distance to our house. I walked over when Kay was at work. It is a good fit. I impressed them with my deep knowledge of literature and books. Almost immediately my passion for published material became evident and I got hired on the spot. Serendipity! This is a good omen for sure. My resolve to execute my plan is back. I am happy that I dodged a bullet; and Kay is happy that I was not up to weaseling my way into lethargy and laziness as she always believes that I will opt for, given half a chance.

Border's is the ideal place for me. They do not mind that when I do something online I have to use my left hand to type, which takes a lot longer to do. Everything is macro-keyed into single stroke functions and most of that which is not can be abbreviated. I can field all customer and staff questions that come my way on the floor with confidence. It took me the better part of a week to get to learn their system of requisitions, pricing, specials, sales, ad campaigns, and customer complaints. It is all cut and dried, and everything comes down from the central headquarters in memos and clear instructions. I try to follow them to the letter. Being pleasant to everyone is a chore for me but my mild manner and self-effacing nature appear to do the trick. I do not offend anyone including unreasonable customers. If I run into a snag with any customer my standard tactic is

"Let me find out about that?"

I go to the floor manager and ask. I then convey the message to the customer with demure efficiency. This however is not intended to last very long. The position is temporary and I am using this as a transitional step to my real goal at the Census Bureau. Furthermore, with the rise of e-books, online sales, and access to all kinds of media, the traditional mode of bookselling is on the decline. This became evident sooner than I anticipated. When I went into my third month review for a potential hire as fulltime staff, I was told that they would no longer need my services. In other words, I am fired due to personnel cuts. It stinks but I only have to feign disappointment.

Now, I want to move on to a D.C. job that can tide me over until when the Census Bureau job opens up. In this light, even the two week severance period is too long. It simply allows me to get out of the house to hunt a new job. Yet, I still need to have an excuse to go to D.C.

HERMIT CRAB - Sail A'non

HERMIT CRAB - Sail A'non

Four
Persistence

This morning, I am overwhelmed with the thought that, so far, I have made very little progress towards my goal. Despite a fractured elbow, a firing, and lots of downtime, I have gotten nowhere close to my goal. The ringing of the phone woke me up from my doldrums. Much to my surprise it is Mr. Nada.

"Hey Ed; how ya'do'in?"

He used exaggerated colloquialisms to make up for his thick Arabic accent.

"You took such a nasty spill the other day that you didn't even stop in for a chat."

That was weeks ago, and this is uncharacteristic of him to call just to ask how I am doing.

"I'm okay; it's okay. I'm coming along nicely. It's just a small fracture."

"Listen, after I saw you that day. Y'know, you lying on the floor like that, ha, ha! (He is trying to be pleasantly humorous.) I remembered that the Zoning Office needs someone like you. They are rewriting some sections of the ordinance; the sanitation sections."

I pretend to like his humor: "Ha, ha! Yes that was some way to reconnect wasn't it?"

"Are you interested in this job? But it is part time."

"Yes, I am interested. I am working at Border's now but it is a temporary thing, until I get my bearings, you know..."

"Oh, you brainy bookworm you; I bet you love that job."

"To tell you the truth it is frustrating to be among so many books and not own any of them. I am getting tired of shuffling between the manager and customers, who have unending demands. I much rather be at the Zoning Office."

"This is not a regular office job. It's consult'n. They need you to do interpretation of some data that they have on refuse collection and disposal patterns for the last 50 years. Brainy-one, this is just up your alley."

It was a no brainer. I was getting closer to official records of real citizens of DC. It is better than sales records at Border's. Saeed's habit of calling me brainy goes back to the time when I used to work for him. It is a foreign-corny phrase with a touch of endearment that makes it alright. There is not much of an IQ challenge at the R&R department of the Zoning Office. Most employees just push paper and click keyboards. I was the "brainy" fish in a small pond full of ignoramuses.

Saeed is the exception He is as smart as they come but is hampered by cultural disadvantages. He is a first generation émigré from Lebanon. He says he studied landscape architecture at the American University in Beirut in its heyday, in the early 80's, when Beirut was considered the Paris of the Middle East. He came to Pratt Institute to study Oriental Architecture, a program designed to accommodate students from East of the 30th Meridian. He earned his degree specializing in urban and regional planning and found an entry position in the Montgomery County's Planning Office; mostly inspecting drawings submitted for building permits and stamping them for further processing by the zoning and records people.

One of the reasons he likes me is due to my short stint, years ago, at the University of Maryland's Architecture and Urban Design College, before I had decided that I was not the designer type. He regarded this episode in my life a valiant effort against odds and constantly intimated his empathy with my predicament, from his elevated position of one who has succeeded.

His upbringing in Lebanon gave him special skills to function well within the slow, repetitive, and soulless work patterns characteristic at the

Planning Office. He endured the drudgery with good humor and Zen-like patience. In spite of his accent, Arabic lineage, and brown skin, which often are the butt of even his-own self-deprecating humor, he rose to administrative ranks rapidly. His jokes and offbeat cultural anecdotes amused the staff and added color to the lifeless ethos that was pervasive at the office.

His Christian faith was also an asset. When I worked for him years ago, he would introduce me to people with a roaring laugh: "Ed here and I get along much better than Anwar and Menachem ever did."

"Ok, Mr. Nada. What do I do next?"

"Just come by tomorrow and I'll get you introduced, brainy-one, ha, ha!"

Serendipity! After a shaky start, my stars are finally lining up just the way I like it. I anticipate that I will enjoy the consulting job much better than my opportunity at Border's. It is part time, yet better suited to my background and interests. It garners more respect, at least in Kay's eyes. To a degree, this will mitigate her paranoia. All of this shifting around will, no doubt, over-stimulate her over-suspicious mind. In any event, I put these speculations aside and rolled up my sleeves – left sleeve anyway.

On the first day at work with Saeed, they issued an official state-government property Toshiba laptop for my use even from off-locations including my home. I got a Wi-Fi internet line hooked up and claimed a permanent location in one corner of the master bedroom where I used to park my stuff. Now I can do a lot of web searching of government sites and demographic records, with impunity and complete privacy. I have the best cover for my search of the vacant shell.

Realizing that this is a legitimate consulting task, Kay shifted gears and became merely sarcastic; referring to my new job as another one of my "temporary triumphs bridging unemployment checks." Since I have the freedom to go to D.C. when I want, and do a lot of online research from home, I do not mind the verbal abuse. It is only temporary.

Like all good things this also quickly came to an end. I completed my final report for the Zoning Board within the allocated time and budget. The project deadline and budget were quite strict and I ended my short flirtation with a "career" in government consultancy within several weeks of my phone conversation with Saeed.

Next, I took a job at the Coroner's Office. My application to the Census Bureau was still pending and the start of work was months off. I had responded to an ad for a starting position at the Coroner's. My previous work in government jobs and reading writing and research qualifications exceeded their minimum requirements. The one blemish in my resume is the frequent moves from job to job. I compensated by getting solid letters of recommendation from Border's, the Zoning Office and AVA. Plus my elbow injury that forced me out of a job was sufficient explanation to persuade the doubters – except Kay of course. I would gladly laze around at home but this new position should get me closer to death records, a crucial piece of my research.

I have to learn how this all works; what is entailed in the Coroner's records; who has access to them; how and at what frequency are these records updated; and what are the transactions with other government offices?

My first impression of the Office of the Chief Medical Examiner of Washington D.C. has been surprisingly positive. There are no encounters with cadaver lying on marble tables, with their brains spilled out, intestines hanging down, and toe tags sticking up. For a split second, I have another flashback to my basement with George in a surgeon's mask and scrubs bending over a table with books that are squirming in agony.

I'm sure there must be some section of this building where this sort of thing takes place but I am on the records section on the third floor. The building is a lot less drab than the Zoning Office. It is right on DuPont Circle, one of the liveliest parts of D.C. Even though my cubby is at the back of the building, I take every opportunity to sneak out to Starbucks, occupying a pizza slice of a building right on the Circle.

My boss, Ms. Boykowycz, for whom I had the most respect among all of the people I worked under, is erudite, pleasant and efficient. I feel that we connected intellectually during my interview. She must have felt similarly about me as our relationship is respectful and unpretentious. My responsibilities include keeping the database well stocked with accurate information. By now, I am comfortable using database systems and anticipating downstream issues in data entry and retrieval.

One day, more out of curiosity than anything else, I walked down to the coroners "workbench" area, so to speak. I was checking something about one of the unfortunate customers in the morgue. I did not encounter any overexposed, gruesome, biological parts, but it was cold, repulsive, and eerie. It reminded me of the reasons why I did not try to be a doctor. I made a mental note that when it came time to quit this job I have the best excuse to convince Kay that I would not be doing it due to impulsion or otiosity.

I neither wish to provoke Kay's ire any further nor disappoint Emily (Ms. Boykowycz). At the moment, I care about her more than any other woman in my life. While this is all quite platonic, I can imagine her being a part of Robert's life. Apparently this infatuation with Emily has translated into behaviors that Kay recognized for what it is. She has become impatient, if not jealous, of hearing Emily's name or descriptions of things that I do for her. With my pathetic appearance and quicksand of a brain, I'm sure she does not deem me capable of luring another woman into an amorous relationship. Yet, her female instincts sense that there is more here than meets the eye. I believe she has worked herself into an uncertain state of jealousy.

My search for the vacant shell did not yield a good result, so far, but taught me a couple of important things. First of all, there is no silver bullet to solve my problem. I will have to combine information from many different sources and fill in the missing pieces.

The kind of information I am looking for is not at any single place. Some of the most critical pieces of information are not found in the accessible public databases. Those that are in specialized databases require clearances that are hard to get. Dead people recorded at the Coroner's are voided from the world of the living in their entirety; they do not leave vacant shells behind. To find a vacant shell suitable for me, I have to start by comparing these death records against those of the Census Bureau.

When the position at the Census Bureau, on 25th Street, opened up, I jumped at the opportunity. This branch office is only a mile from the Coroner's, along New Hampshire Avenue, near George Washington University, where I had taken some Law classes when I was an undergraduate at U of M. This brings back memories of youth and vitality – which I consider as a good omen.

The Census Bureau turned out to be the ideal place for my research. It's business is to collect demographic information about everyone, This is the wide net with which I can start my search, layering on top of it filters to eliminate what is not of interest until I reach the core set of candidates for my vacant shell. I will have to obtain each of these filters from other sources like the Vital Records Office, Social Security Administration,

Internal Revenue Service, even Immigration and Naturalization.

During one of my excursions to scout out what other data resources would be available to me, I stopped at the US Federal Archives. I must have spent three hours committing to memory key information about the type and scope of governmental reports and appendixes containing detailed demographic information. I am afraid to take notes on paper for fear that I might be discovered before I transform myself into Robert. Learning titles dates and scope of dozens of government documents has strained my brain, beyond its normal capacity to hold rote information. So I decided to walk over to the Old Post Office pavilion where they have reasonably priced kosher deli sandwiches,.

It's a pleasant walk on Constitution Avenue along the Mall and then on 12th Street. It helped me take stock and assess my progress. It was close to rush hour, which is dreadful, and the place was already teeming with government employees. This is where they shot a memorable scene in the movie "No Way Out" with Kevin Costner. A bit of trivia I learned from Annone who is a film freak. This building must be one of the most successful projects of re-gentrification in the 80s. It has a magnificent atrium space lined with commercial and retail stores. A large number of restaurants alongside food vendors located on the ground and lower floors cater to many tastes and budgets. Government employees located around the building help provide substantial patronage for these retailers.

The atrium is restored exquisitely, I believe by Rouse Co. of the Baltimore's Harbor Place, and Boston's Faneuil Hall fame. In any event, it is one of those nationally known developers taking a rundown property, fixing it up and making a sweet profit when the marketing plan works as intended. These projects are subsidized through public funds in order to encourage urban development and improve the tax base. Profits are usually guaranteed for those who have capital and expertise. We the average folk end up securing their ventures through patronage. It is rumored that Trump Enterprises will take the next shot at this property, as a hotel or a convention center.

I walked around the mezzanine thinking about Trump Enterprises, taking in the retail stores, and admiring the well-dressed downtown crowd rushing about their destinations. I moved slowly to the head of the grand stairs which leads to the food court. I tried to imagine the chase scene in "No Way Out" which takes place right at this spot; the

FBI goons chasing an illegal émigré from Ethiopia, leaping over food carts and falling all over the stairs, when the image I was conjuring was pierced by a familiar face.

"Hello Ed. "

"Hi Saeed."

"How ya'do'in?"

"I was just trying to figure out if Kevin Costner would come running up these stairs any moment now." I was trying to be facetious not realizing that Saeed was not a movies guy.

"Kevin who?"

"You know the movie; no way out?" I was trying to change the subject so that I would not have to explain why I was here at this time. I keep finding myself explaining things to Saeed that I did not want or need to.

"Y'know, I am not much for movies. Can you imagine paying $25-30 a person, not to mention….?" He went into the standard accounting of how much movies cost these days, which everyone has heard countless times.

"Anyhow; how are you?" asked Saeed.

I replied: "OK I guess."

"You know I got a very nice complement from the Zoning Office for your report on the sanitation people."

"Yeah? Thank you."

"Maybe I should ask these security guards if they know about movies that were shot here. It is a pretty spectacular space." I'm still trying to change the subject.

"What are you do'in here anyways?"

My attempt to digress did not work. We're back to square one. I can't tell him why I went to the archives. When I execute my plan, he is a likely subject for the investigation of my whereabouts. Kay knows Saeed and that he has been looking out for me all these years. Once, during those early days when I used to work for him, he and his wife even came to dinner.

I had to provide a cover that Saeed would buy: "I am getting some information for one of Jay's school projects, on civil liberties."

This is partially true; a standard explanation I had prepared ahead of time just for such an occasion. Then I improvised, for the sake of making it more authentic.

"In fact it would be very helpful if he could contact you with a few questions."

This was flattery and Saeed was pleased enough to take it seriously.

"How old is your son now? Last time I saw him he was a toddler or somethi'n."

"He is 13.5"

"Wow, that's a lot'a years. What's he do'in writ'n about civic affairs at his young age? Oh I get it, he must be brainy-junior."

"Something like that..." He was right about Jay but I did not want to seem conceited by agreeing with him too enthusiastically.

"Sure I'll talk to him. Have him call me tomorrow after work. You still have my number don't you? But wait I changed jobs; I have a position at the Census Bureau, central HQ. Here take this."

He carefully removed a business card from his wallet and handed it to me. The card was brand new, without any of the usual wear you see in those that have been kept in a sweaty, curved wallet too long.

"How did this happen? Zoning office seemed such a good fit for you."

"The ole glass ceiling... it is not just for ladies y'know; it is also for foreigners. And the sanitation people are like a pack of fuddy duddies. They stick together. I wasn't getting anywhere with them."

"Besides, the Census Bureau HQ is a full time operation."

With empathy, I added. "Also don't they need people with ethnic color and knowledge for insights into minorities and ethnic outcasts?"

Saeed confirmed, "Brown in this case is good, very good. Your son – what's his name – oh, Jay, OK, have him call me."

My mind raced from the movies, to ethnic glass ceilings, and settled on the card in my hand.

> Saeed Nada, Assistant Director
> Office of Regional Data Coordination
> U.S. Census Bureau
> 600 Silver Hill Road
> Washington, DC 20233

I wanted to rub my eyes to make sure I was seeing right. The opportunities a job like this can present for accessing the hidden corners of the Census Bureau data are enormous. I have to nurture my relationship with Saeed now more than ever. It's a good thing that he likes me.

He seems to be reading my thoughts: "This is such a coincidence. I just got a position at the West Regional Office here in D.C. We must be destined to be together"

"Isn't that the truth? So, how do you like D.C. Saeed? Did you make the move?"

"No it is such a hassle to find a house, sell a house, pack and unpack, just to save some commute time."

"Don't remind me of moves, some of my most cathartic experiences in life involve moving a house."

Saeed seemed to ignore my pathos, "I bet you are doing just as good a job here as you were doing at the Zoning office."

"Yes, but to be honest I have some problems with the data I'm processing, I wonder if I can come by to see you someday to pick your brain."

"Okay, why don't we do that?"

"I will come with Jay. Like you say, we'll kill two birds."

"Is sometime next week fine?"

"Sure, Jay's work is not so urgent."

In fact it does not exist. I'll have to find some excuse to go alone. There is no sense dragging Jay into my disingenuous ploys.

"Listen, I got 'a go"

"Good seeing you Saeed."

"Ok, bye." He turned around and left.

I hope I did not piss him off with my chit chat. I walked over to the kosher deli stand and ordered pastrami on rye. Perched up on one of those tall stools that mimic the shape of the tall, round tables by which they are placed and I started eating. Adrenalin always makes me hungry. For the first time, I am convinced that I will ride out into the sunset in the near future.

I feel restless. I found myself stuffing my face vigorously, as if the minutes I could shave off the clock now would help foreshorten Ed's life and extend that of Robert's.

Five
Toil

I found this on the web.

"The Twenty-Second United States Census, known as Census 2010 and conducted by the Census Bureau, determined the resident population of the United States on April 1, 2010, to be 321,421,906, an increase of 11.2% over the 281,421,906 persons enumerated during the 2000 Census."

Now, based on this, if the same rate of population increase were to be realized, the population of the US, in 2016, should be 348,839,763. I figure, the vast majority, say 99.999% of this, will be of no use to me. This is a needle in a hay stack problem; since all that I need is just one empty record, no more, no less. Besides, I have some powerful tools at my disposal now. As a midlevel data entry supervisor, I have access to all of the census data regardless of the jurisdiction of our regional office. Partitioning the data into regional compartments is counterproductive since the final census data has to subsume all of those compartments.

It would be easier to search this huge central database for a certain profile if it were indexed trough regional, governmental, geographic, and demographic filters. This would require using multiple criteria to sort it into smaller and smaller parts. So I decided to get a head start with my haystack problem.

The first filter I applied is to eliminate females. Next, I filtered out all below 50 and above 55 years of age. Finally, I did the temporary Social Security number filter, typically assigned to students, visiting scholars, who do not have permanent resident status. This is not easy for a humanities-type such as I but I must do all that is necessary. By the time this is all over I'll be a real Renaissance Man. I plugged the filter code into the App and waited a while. The number of entries in the subset my filters spit out came to 1,832,412 individual records. I still have to eliminate millions of records before I can whittle this down to singularity.

I seem to be fighting this battle between singularity and plurality. I need a unique existence in the haystack of multitudes. Our genetic code is a singular pattern that defines us as a species while affording unique attributes to each individual member of the superset. Call it evolution, call it intelligent design, call it what you will, it manages to take the mundane into sublime. I am trying to reverse engineer this divine web of connections with much more primitive tools than those at the disposal of our creators. I have census filters and a huge database. I need to go from this morass of records to a singularity that is a perfect fit for my specifications. If I had possession of our creators' divine tools, I could design Robert with much greater ease than clumsily sorting through filters.

I saved the result I obtained in a folder with an obscure name for future access. I am hoping to obtain a few handfuls of individuals' records from which to pick the finalists. These are the people who would pass my basic three or four filters and in addition meet the empty record criterion – either homeless, deceased without id, left the country never to be found, or had illegal alien status to start with.

The trouble is not all of these records would be a good fit for my needs. For personal reasons I want an American born. For practical reasons he should be around my age with similar family background, Jewish descent, and moderately educated – although I believe I am educated enough to feign incompetence, if it came to that. The likelihood that I will find all of these attributes in at least one out of millions of individual candidates is very small.

The Jewish population of the US is 1.88%. Statistically speaking, only a fraction of one person out of the finalist individuals would be a Jew. I have to eliminate this requirement all together and concentrate on the other factors. Once I become Robert, I can always convert to Judaism. With my present knowledge of the faith this would not be so difficult.

I feel that the demographic difference between Ed and Robert should be only in name and official papers. Practically speaking, this would certainly come handy when I provide family histories to dentists, doctors, and in social settings. The better the fit between backgrounds the less of a chance for slip ups. From an emotional stand point, this is a serious issue. What I'm attempting is not just a mechanical swap, as if I'm pouring tea into Robert's saucer from the kettle of entire humanity. It is a significant rearrangement of one's inner being. Every time I respond to the name Robert, use a credit card or a driver's license, explain something about my background, and say something personal, I will be living a lie. I will have done all of this to end up playing the lead role in a fraud. But I do not have a way out of this. I need to make Robert as much like Edward as possible.

My mother was a diabetic. She lost both legs to her disease and was partially blind when her heart stopped after her seventh surgery in a span of 18 months. Doctors could not arrest the gangrene and the rupturing of arteries that had invaded her lower extremities. Until her final demise, she did not have any major health problems.

Years ago, when she went through her menopause she was depressed out of her skull. She stopped jamming and baking for a good long time, two hobbies she shared with Kay. It was not easy for her to accept a Catholic daughter-in-law. If it weren't for the long hours they spent together during our courtship, jamming and baking, I do not believe I would ever be able to overcome her objections to Kay.

Towards the end Jay and I were the only visitors of my mom during our bi-weekly family events. Kay kept coming up with excuses. I believe secretly she was extracting revenge for the resentment my mom harbored towards her during the early phase of our pre-nuptials.

My dad outlived my mother by six months. After such a long marriage a man without his wife is pretty much lost. He tried to manage himself at the condo as best as he could but he also had serious health problems. As a child he was asthmatic. I inherited my respiratory problems from his side of the family.

Over the years he was able to keep them under control but never got rid of them all together. He also was troubled by an enlarged prostate, which made him get up to empty his bladder in the middle of the night for as long as I can remember. It never developed into anything as lethal as cancer but it was a source of discomfort for him and my mom, the true dimensions of which I learned after my mom passed away.

In one of our heart to heart conversations about life, death and all that is in between my dad confided in me that his prostate problems were due to curtailed sexual activity, hinting at my mother's prudishness and reserve in the bed. This is one of the reasons why I ended up as the only child. One was enough for my mom as it was for Kay.

When my father passed away earlier this year he was 78, three years older than my mom. He had a massive heart attack. I call it the revenge of the pastrami on rye. All of those matzo balls and gefilte fish could not save him from hardening arteries and plaque. He had high cholesterol and never exercised. After each meal, he took catnaps on the couch watching TV. He was also an avid reader of the newspaper from cover to cover.

I believe he must be the one who instilled the love of reading in me. While he was obstinately frugal with other purchases, he never turned me down when I wanted to have a book. My mother's endless requests for new furniture were met with one excuse after another until all excuses expired at about the same time as nearly did her life. My parents bought a new dining-living set two years before she passed away. Since she spent most of her time in and out of hospitals and nursing homes during that time, she was not able to enjoy any of it, which Kay and I now do, in our new abode, on her behalf.

I woke up this morning with an epiphany. When I went to bed last night, I was still thinking about Jay's assignment for history. He was researching the Ottomans who created an Empire out of semi-autonomous fiefdoms that collected taxes and young military recruits for the empire while allowing a relatively free reign in other matters. They created a good match between a top down authoritative order for military, civic, and infrastructure matters that fit bottom up considerations well enough, if not perfectly, and lasted for over 500 years.

I have been thinking about my problem as a top-down view. I started with the entire US population and tried to whittle it down to one person. This is like trying to catch that perfect singular water drop from water gushing out of hundreds of fire hydrant spigots at once. Instead, I should start with the right spigot and reduce the flow to a drip. I should start with real people and try to fit them to my vision.

I began to take off a little early from work and spent some time volunteering at the National Coalition for the homeless at P and 23rd, a short walk from my place of work. The center seeks volunteers to do clerical work, food service, dishwashing or distribution of clothing. I signed up for kitchen duty to have direct contact with the unfortunate souls that came in each day for an early dinner. I was known there as Gregg Bell. I served food, helped prepare the menu, monitored serving sizes, even peeled potatoes – everything except cooking, which I despised.

I got to know a range of personalities most of whom were mental cases, alcoholics, drug addicts and dropouts. Some are suitable subjects. For instance, Cato looked in his 60s but his real age was probably closer to 50. He is a hardcore addict and mostly keeps to himself. When I tried to strike a conversation with him, he eyed me with suspicion. I was not sure if this was due to my social awkwardness or his chemically induced paranoia.

Eventually, I was able to gain his trust. He did not seem to have family or friends and claimed to be an orphan. He was from Washington, Pennsylvania and had spent some time at the mental ward of the hospital system in Pittsburgh. He made his way to D.C. to escape the cold of the lake effects in the winter. I had a sneaking suspicion that his warped mind latched onto the similarity in the names of the two locations, which could have been a source of comfort.

I said, "D.C. is the center of the world."

He agreed, "Yeah."

I was trying to find an acknowledgement of this hyperbole without talking down at him. "It is the capital of the nation."

He threw a glance of abject belittlement in my direction. Ordinarily he kept his eyes away when he talked. This was a deliberate warning that he was not to be patronized. For Cato to become available for my plan, he will have to die, be buried as an "unidentified decedent," and not be matched with any missing persons.

During my research at the National Archives I learned about *NamUs* – National Missing and Unidentified Persons – system that was created by the Department of Justice to match missing persons with unidentified remains. There are a total of 4077 missing person cases and 6617 unidentified persons in the NamUs database. This means that there are 2540 available for me. In death, Cato would fall into one of these spots; however, he could be matched later through the NamUs system. While the chances of this match are low and the percentage of cases unresolved quite high I still cannot take a chance. What if I move into Cato's shell only to have *NamUs* declare me deceased?

Just for the sport of it, I logged into NamUs' Missing Persons database, which is open to public access in order to increase the number of matching cases, Cato is not there. Besides, while Cato's health is a mess there is no guaranty that he will die anytime soon, and I am not about to contemplate murder. There is a limit to how far I will go. Also, I knew next to nothing about Cato's background. At one point I had asked him about where he was born and he looked at me with piercing eyes, the second time I asked he made eye contact with me before I finished my query.

"Why; do you want to collect my inheritance?"

What was a casual, almost facetious, remark hit so close to home that it completely unnerved me? I mumbled something inane and neither he nor I broached the subject ever again. My attempt to develop a case through the bottom-up approach is not working that well either.

I tried to befriend and gather information about other regulars of the shelter with similar dead ends. I am getting the feeling that they are beginning to consider me with suspicion.

Their responses are much too curt, followed by utter avoidance. Every now and then, when I approach someone with a question I feel the invisible mark of piercing glances on my back. It is time to quit the shelter. Once more, I am stuck and discouraged, as the census work is beginning to shift to the field more and more. Before the pressure on database applications starts building up again, I decided to take off for a week to have our annual family vacation at Cape May. It was not difficult for Kay to synchronize her annual leave at AVA. Mr. Ostergaard treated her well, besides work was slow during the summer.

HERMIT CRAB - Sail A'non

Six
Aplomb

"Yes dear, I am driving slowly. Look, everyone is passing me."

…

"No, I'm not going 70 miles. From your angle it looks like that, the needle is elevated and it lines up with the wrong marker. I meant to say, from your side it looks …"

…

"Jay, do not interrupt when mom and I are talking."

…

"I thought you wanted me to explain… "

…

"Fine, I'll concentrate on driving and you talk."

That's what I should have done in the first place. Jay and Kay were going over the things we forgot to pack. I packed a small suitcase of clothing, essentials and a couple of good books to read. I chose lighter material suitable for the vacation mood: *Conspirata* by Robert Harris and *Blink* by Gladwell. This I thought is a good dry run for how I will be packing when I depart for my empty shell.

In the previous years at Cape May I enjoyed reading the Robert Graves' Trilogy starting with *I Claudius.* It gave me a chance to reexamine the origins of Jesus' rise to prominence in the 2nd and 3rd Centuries, from a fictionalized lay perspective. During our earlier Cape May days, I had read Eco's *Name of the Roes, Foucault's Pendulum* and *Island of the Day After.*

In *Island,* Eco has created an alter ego for his hero, which sets up an interesting parallel to my dual identity conflict. I reminded myself to stop confusing fact and fiction, something that has caused endless problems for me throughout life. I will have to find comparable semi-fictional sources to make my escape a bit more enjoyable, otherwise destined to be a torturous trip on Dachshund.

"Ed! For the last time, did you remember to take your swimming trunks and sun block? You've gone into a trans again" Kay was yelling.

"I was just concentrating on …"

"I have no idea where you go, when you're like this. I am not spending anything on new trunks and sun block for you."

"I think …"

"Once again, you'll end up looking bizarre with your lily white skin turning crimson adorned with a lobster-red nose."

"I think I got them."

"Are you sure? I don't even want to be around when you look like that or even worse."

"I am planning to wear slacks and a shirt at the beach. What's the use of putting on all that sun block that wears off in an hour or two anyway? You can protect yourself perfectly well and save money too."

"Ha, ha! " Kay let loose one of her fake, high decibel laughs.

"Jay can you imagine your dad looking like that at the beach? Ha, ha! I think you should also wear socks and shoes…"

"As a matter of fact I was going to wear socks since the top of the feet are the first to go under the subtending angle of the sun being so vertical at noon..."

"Subtend what? What fucking gibberish are you cooking up now? You'll not only be a sight for sore eyes but will even be ridiculed by seagulls, cick-gaak, cick-gaak, eek, eek, eek"

Her attempt to imitate seagulls was intended as ridicule but turned out to be a great release for our nerves. The tension was broken. Jay chimed in with almost a perfect imitation of Jake.

"cick-gaak, cick-gaak."

"Didn't Jonathan Livingston Seagull write this seagull story?" Kay was not an avid reader; she was confusing the name of the lead character with the name of the author.

"It is by Richard Bach." Jay responded.

I did not want to rub in Kay's ignorance of classics by American literary greats, and changed the subject. "I would also like to find a tent or umbrella to stay under."

"Why do you even bother to go to the beach if you are going to be fully dressed sitting under a tent. Wimp out at home! Jay and I will enjoy the ocean on your behalf."

"I'm trying to avoid skin cancer. As a child I had a very bad case of sunburn."

Jay added. "Yes, it was at Atlantic City."

I went ahead and answered Kay's earlier question. "I like to be with you honeybunch, even if I'm in a tent."

This was enough to disarm her.

Jay seized the moment. "It'll be fine mom. I like dad to be with us. What kind of family vacation would it be without him?"

Kay received the retort with silence. She was outnumbered, not that that really ever mattered. It provided just enough counter-traction that she let the radio and road sounds consume the space in the family van.

Jay is the only soul who has insight into my private ambitions; how I came to my own as a teen in the 70s; wanted to become a rock-and-roll drummer but never picked up the sticks; how I wanted to become an accomplished writer some day; or that I would make a great CEO given half a chance. He is well versed in my lamentations about the commercialization of everyday life. I know he does not believe everything I say but he takes it in with care. He is a great listener. He is in his sponge stage. I am confident that he will turn into a fine young man; too bad I won't be there to see it.

Jay started murmuring a tune we used to sing on our way to Cape May when he was a pre-teen. Gradually we joined in and transformed the van into a jovial chorus on wheels:

"Alouette, jaunte alouette,
Alouette, jaunte Alouette
Alouette, je te plumerai
Je te plumerai la tête ..
Je te plumerai la tête
Et la tête .... Et la tête
Alouette ... Alouette
O-o-o-oh..."
And so on.

This was a song I had learned one summer when I was travelling with my parents to France, to visit relatives and attend a wedding. They had debated endlessly whether we could afford the trip and saved for six months to pull it off. It was almost family honor to make it to the wedding as relatives from all over the world were attending. One of my most vivid memories as a child is singing this song with my cousins. There were a whole slew of them dressed in fancy outfits running around in a large room littered with confetti and balloons.

Many years later, when I learned the meaning of the lyrics, I was disappointed:

"Little skylark, lovely little skylark;
little lark, I will pluck your feathers off;
I'll pluck the feathers off your head;
I'll pluck the feathers off your head; off
your head - off your head; little lark,
little lark; O-o-o-o-oh;"

The lyrics repeated the same refrain for beak, neck, wings, back, legs, and tail of the poor devil. I always thought that it was some romantic or at least affectionate song about a young girl, not poultry. The violent acts depicted in the song pretty much shattered my long held childhood memories. Sometimes, ignorance IS bliss.

Cape May brings back feelings of tranquility and nostalgia and tranquility. For the last five years, we have been renting the same apartment carved out of the first floor of a Victorian house on the outskirts of town. It is a short drive to the beach and center of town that makes it affordable to rent.

The apartment is spacious and has all of the old time charm one could expect for the rent we pay. Kay and I share a bedroom equipped with two doubles. We have been sleeping separately for a number of years now. We both snore and provide mutual disruption for each other. The distance between the beds provides a bit of a buffer, at least psychologically.

Jay gets the master bedroom since it has a compact bathroom. We use the bathroom off of the hallway that is larger and equipped with a double vanity. I get to use Jay's bathroom when I pee. Kay is annoyed with the splashing of urine and my leaving the seat up on occasion.

The kitchen is large enough to accommodate a table where we eat our meals. Didn't I already tell you that Kay can bake and jam like and angel but is a terrible cook; and so am I? We end up ordering a lot of pizza and prepare spaghetti with red sauce. We can afford to eat out twice during our stay; one of them on the final evening of our vacation, which is meant to be the crowning of our summer break.

But it usually serves as the reminder that there is little to look forward to for a good long time.

The tension accompanying this idea is usually sufficient to throw us into minor arguments, usually about what we each should order and how much each dish costs. We trip all over our clever strategies for making unusual combinations of the menu items in order to get more for less. This usually backfires, and we get things that we didn't want and spend an amount we did not intend. This leads to circular accusations about being misled by casually offered comments while ordering. But at the end, after all is said and done there is a sense of closure that our mission is complete and the inevitable is behind us.

By the third day of our vacation, I was totally relaxed. I was dressed in my standard beach attire, slacks, long sleeve shirt, sun glasses, and a wide brim safari hat, no sun block; completely absorbed in *Conspirata*. By the time I realized that I did not have my socks on and the sun had penetrated through my paper thin, white skin along the top of my feet, it was too late. At the end of the day, the area above my toe nails and below my ankles were like raw meat.

At first, I tried to conceal this and splashed on a lot of Aloe Vera. The only kind we had was spiked with mint and seemed to make my pain even worse, either that or the sunburn was beginning to show its full effect. I was in agony and could hardly have anything touch my feet, including the hem of my slacks. I was walking around like a Japanese woman with bound feet inserted in lobster shells. Kay spotted me trying to negotiate the hallway leading to the living room.

"How can you be so inconsiderate? As if it was not enough that you looked like an Arabic Sheik; you could not manage the keep properly protected."

Usually her tirades have a short cycle, peak off in a few minutes and tail off during a few more. This time she was gaining more inertia with each passing minute. Pitching insults left and right, looking for the Aloe bottle not realizing that I had already taken it from the bathroom cabinet; and calling me a complete moron intentionally ruining her vacation.

"This will spoil everything. How are you going to do anything? Now, I have to do everything for us. Why can't you use sunblock like everyone else? You cheap bastard! Like father like son." This last comment was the final straw and it brought something over me that is not usually the case.

"I'm fucking tired of hearing your endless yapping. Ok, I am a moron to do this. Will you just shut the crap up?"

For a moment Kay looked like she was about to search the room for the ventriloquist who put those words in my mouth. Realizing that I actually did say them, she froze. Took the first thing that she found on the kitchen table, which mercifully, and ironically, was the mostly used up sunblock bottle, and threw it at me with all her might. It bounced off of the wall behind me and fell harmlessly on my shoulder.

"You, asshole, I should have never married you!" With these words she went into the bedroom and slammed the door.

Jay and I had a couple of peanut butter and jelly sandwiches for dinner, and slept in the master bedroom on the queen sized bed. We spoke little, other than trying to comfort each other with little or no success. Later, Jay went into Kay's room. There was little I could hear other than a few inaudible exclamations that resembled Kay's voice at high pitch. Jay emerged a few minutes later looking gloomy. He fell asleep from physical and emotional exhaustion. I was sure that the pain would keep me awake all night long but somehow I must have lost consciousness shortly after.

When I woke up, miraculously the pain was gone, it must be the globs of Aloe I put on my feet the night before. It was remarkable. I had a comfortable inner calm.

The ceiling was aglow with fuchsia, turquoise, and khaki swirls reflecting off of the chandelier. Everything seemed to be subsumed by a glow of effervescence. Tranquility was a lead colored cloud, through which a formation began to emerge: it was Kay's face. I had never seen her like this before. Her eyes were red and bulging; her bonny cheeks were sunken more than usual. Her teeth were peering between her thin, parted lips. She seemed neither angry nor upset, but there was something unsettling, menacing about her. I wanted to ask her what the matter was. Then it dawned on me: she looked evil.

"You fucking shit bag!" she screamed. "Get the fuck up. You've really done it this time, you scumbag! I'll cut your balls off and stick them up your ass! Yeah, that will finally do it; you will be able to shit balls."

As she yelled her face became even more contorted and began to transform into an insect like formation before my eyes. All of her skin turned red and then brown. A brownish grey hue began to ooze from between her teeth. The effervescence began to pixelate, becoming a swarm of mosquitoes that swirled around her head and the chandelier before covering the entire surface of the ceiling that was now cloud-like. The colors of the room had turned into a dirty brown; the highlights became black holes sucking out all of the oxygen. I began to suffocate. A burning sensation overtook my lungs. I opened my mouth to apologize that I yelled at her, but no sound came out.

I kept staring at her. Her head was surrounded by the brown foam-like cloud flowing from her mouth that lifted her beautiful brown hair into a lock dancing in midair. This created a halo around her head adding a grotesque angelic quality to the demonic features of her face that inched ever so closer to mine. I opened my mouth to scream but instead inhaled a lung-full of the brown foam. The burning sensation in my lungs intensified branching out into my body, gradually reaching all of my extremities. I was consumed with it. I closed my eyes and tried to move my face away. I seemed to be paralyzed by the effect of the foam. I jerked my body as violently as I could. My left arm went flying as I rolled and hit Jay on the shoulder. I woke up. Jay was looking at me fearfully. "What's wrong dad?"

I was too terrified and excited to say anything or to go back to sleep. I must have dozed off, before dawn. When I woke up there were normal conversational sounds emanating from the kitchen. I must have stared at the ceiling and the sun's reflection off of the chandelier for what seemed like hours. When I stepped off of my bed the veins of my feet felt like bursting with pressure and pain. I inched my way to the bathroom and then to the kitchen. I discovered a few leftover pancakes and a note from Jay on the table.

We transitioned into the second half of our week with the help of staying at our corners. Our last evening's dinner turned out to be unusually civil and did not sport a big argument. Avoidance behavior was working, and Jay seems to be enjoying his new role as the pinch-hitter filling the void with small talk and occasional comments of warmth towards Kay. I am surprised that he is capable of this much exuberance and political savvy, at once. This worked well for all, reconstructing the week, which otherwise would have been a very unpleasant affair for all.

The dye of my plan to disappear is cast. This is almost a dress rehearsal of the emotional stages I would go through on my last day as Ed; if it were feasible, I could walkout right now and would not even flinch.

HERMIT CRAB - Sail A'non

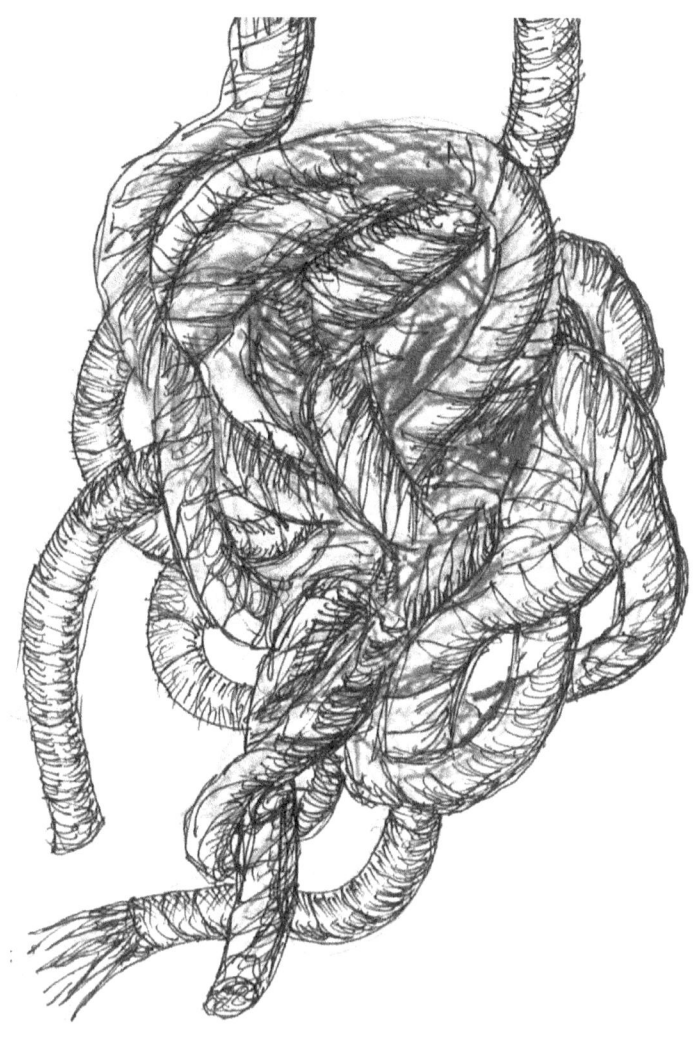

Seven
Nouement

After Cape May, I returned to the Census Bureau with renewed determination. I recalled hearing somewhere that *if you do not manage your circumstances then your circumstances will manage you.*

There was a mountain of data entry sets waiting to be processed. I kept working long hours to devote time to searching for that all illusive empty shell. Kay no longer bothers me or requires detailed explanations when I come home late. "Don't ask, don't tell" is our *modus operandi*. Little by little I am becoming more focused, energetic and hopeful. At times, I feel content; even happy.

If it weren't for the long years of thought that went into it, I could almost retire my plan of exodus as a distant dream. But by now my constitution is engrained with deep longings for Robert and these second-thoughts or regrets are merely fleeting.

I find myself speculating about other people's lives, daydreaming whether they are happy or not based on their address, age, name, co-residents, gender and anything else I can fathom.

I am also talking to others in the office about non-routine cases and anomalies to discover things I don't know about irregularities and the fine points of the system. On a Friday when I was contemplating the progress I was <u>not</u> making, it suddenly happened. I had my breakthrough when I was talking to Chip, the whiz kid, manager of our system. Chip is not one of those with a screw driver in the back pocket. He is a dropout from a prestigious Computer Science program placing him pretty close to being a software engineer. He could write new Apps and diagnose glitches in the system with the skill of a chess master facing 20 opponents at once. He installed the entire system in our branch office.

We are using the Oracle System adapted to government requirements for a series of security levels allowing different operators to independently access the data that they need. I was convinced that I had to learn about these fine points of our database system. As I entered Chip's cubie, his back was turned towards me and he did not know who was there so asked reflexively:

"What do you want, you *bone smuggler*?"

Chip, whose real name was Douglas Brown, which I'm sure he considered too conventional for his taste, is a boisterous little clown in love with cheap humor. If he thought he could get away with it, he would call everyone a bone smuggler to their face; others were targeted only behind their back. When he misjudged someone and got a terse reply or a wicked look he thought twice about these "Chip-shots." Yet owing to the gigantic clout he lugged around due to his enormous software savvy, it did not take too long before he would be forgiven.

"What else can oracle do for us?" I asked.

He never questioned anyone's reasons or motives for asking such questions. He was too eager to spew out all kinds of information that no doubt was overflowing from his overstuffed brain. He rattled off all kinds of jargon, half of which I did not follow.

"There is the 2KTMC; it's the main census info bank. Then there is the state by state breakdown under this ... each state requires different sorting capabilities ... programmed with specialization schema stored in the main Oracle server and retrieved when needed ... the short survey results are in one sub-disk and the long survey forms are entered in another ... statistically extrapolated data is saved separately ... and so is the package that executes the extrapolations."

He continued. "Then there is special stuff that I can use to augment 2KTMC in different ways. DERELICT, clever name huh, I am the godfather of that bone smuggler, stands for Duplication Elimination Restoration Certification Taskforce... I found out that that there was a real taskforce like that decades ago made up of live bone smugglers but it only exists in my digits these days. DERELICT can find duplicate cases collected redundantly by independent field workers, uploaded from various databases, or made whole from partial entries ... it discovers errors by comparing records of a variety of government databases"

I was genuinely puzzled. "Do you mean you can access other databases from DERELICT? I thought that sort of that thing did not happen."

He looked at me sideways feigning pity. "Do you realize who you're talking to? I'm no ordinary bone smuggler, my friend. I can tap into almost any database. I got pals all over town who are incredible bone smugglers."

Bingo! This sounds like the real thing.

While the bone smuggling concept was really annoying and Chip was so juvenile about it that instead of moving on he kept expanding its scope; I decided to fake amusement which is more than he expects or gets under normal circumstances.

"Ha, ha."

"There is a lot of exchange between Census and IRS, INS,, even FBI and CIA, since they get data from us more than we do from them, I can pretty much track down any hapless bone smuggler on any database. This is the way our data was made robust and error free."

According to Chip, this breach between databases could jeopardize the wellbeing of "special-case bone smugglers," which is why all of this had to be kept hush hush. Hence, DERELICT was under the control of the Bureau Director's office. A lot of profile discovery was going on but it was all undercover.

Could all of this be just a boastful fib? Yet, I decided to dig deeper, in case there was something to it.

"What kind of profiling?"

"Let's say we want to know who is really a legit bone smuggler."

"Is that all?"

"We also get queries from FBI, CIA, DHS, you name it. We can id terrorist bone smugglers or weed out other stuff cluttering their databases."

Even if Chip is just blowing smoke this sounds very interesting. If only I could get into DERLICT.

Next morning, I went to see Mr. Nada at the headquarters. I had to wait a while before he came in, no doubt, after having finished his post breakfast Turkish coffee, allotting it its mandatory pace of slurping.

His taste for Turkish coffee is a remnant from his father who had migrated from Egypt where the traditions of coffee as well as many other forms of Middle Eastern folklore date back centuries into the Ottoman times. Saeed always spoke fondly of the times when he and his father drank Turkish coffee prepared by her older sister, after which his mother read their fortunes gazing at the coffee grains left at the bottom of the miniature saucer. Adapting to the work schedules in the States he has his coffee in the morning rather than in the afternoon as is customary in Lebanon.

After the usual pleasantries that were mandatory with Saeed, I came right to the point. "I learned that there is a special application that deals with removing erroneous data entries or some such thing [pretending that I did not know about DERLICT]. Is this true?"

He looked at me with suspicion.

"Who told you that?" I did not skip a beat; I knew if I was going to go anywhere I had to level with him and bank on our rapport and mutual trust.

"Chip."

"Who the hell is he?"

"He is the system analyst at our office. His real name is Douglas. Douglas Brown."

"Oh, the bone smuggler... Brainy, you should know better, half the time, that *bone smuggler* does not know what he is talking about."

He was pleased with his early morning humor at Chips expense.

"Ok, there is a system that we developed here and have allowed our branch offices to use in a limited way on an as needed basis. Chip must be talking about that, it is called DERELICT, but it is not for everyone. It is accessible by top brass only."

"What's the secrecy about it? I just want to de-weed some clutter in our database."

"You know, the census data is for census purposes only. We do not want to have it used for other purposes, or we betray confidentiality, to which we have sworn our solemn pledge."

Sometimes, Saeed can get super-altruistic and hyper-ethical; and there is no getting around it unless you play along. So I looked approvingly without uttering a word.

He continued: "To improve our preparation for accuracy and efficiency in our census work we have to insure trust for aliens and all kinds of vulnerable people Even the president talked about this explicitly in his directive to the Bureau."

Saeed does not miss an opportunity to sound pompous. He was also enjoying speaking to me in feigned confidence.

"Now, how would you like if the word got out that there is more to the census data than the census."

"Mr. Nada, you know me I'm not a talker. I just want to do a better job."

"Brainy, brainy, brainy ... This is all bone smuggler's fault. He let the cat out of the bag. You know you will not be able to access DERELICT, it is out of the question, but I'll let you have read-only privileges; you'll have no other functionality activated with it … other than just looking."

"You can trust me. If Anwar and Menachem can shake hands so can we."

He saw right through my design to win him over, he was a master of such remarks, but this time he did not even bother to respond to it.

"You'll see it is only one way, from outside agencies to us; so there is no leakage from us to anyone else." He was doing damage control.

At this point I did not care what fallout would occur or if Chip got into trouble. I was locked onto my plan like a laser beam. Once I disappeared, all hell can break loose as far as I'm concerned.

Saeed did not hold a top clearance position either but it was high enough to get me the read-only access to DERELICT. He knew how bureaucracy worked well enough. He had me fill out some forms and sign confidentiality papers which were complicated and scary.

Three days after my visit to Mr. Nada's office, I received a memo giving me access to DERELICT with a temporary ID and PWD that had to be verified at the Bureau's secure main server site. These access privileges would expire within two weeks. I decided to do my research quickly and even write a report for Mr. Nada's eyes only indicating the potential benefits of DERELICT to our work. Efficiency in government bureaucracy is not always at the top of the totem pole but who can blame one for trying. At least it makes good PR.

Just by looking at the links at its top layers, I was amazed at the list of external databases accessible from DERELICT. Even though I could neither access most of these nor understand what they were all about. Some of them I recognized readily, EPA (Environmental Protection Agency), HUD (Housing and Urban Development), AID (Agency for International Development), DOD (Department of Defense), and even some unlikely ones like NSF (National Science Foundation), NIH (National Institute of Health), NEA (National Energy Agency), NIST (National Institute of Standards and Technology).

I am like the hungry hobo lusting after the deserts on the window of a bakery shop. Even though my motivation was not seeking piety, atonement, or repentance, like a man about to come out of Yom Kippur, I was salivating over what I was about to do. I accessed the census data through DERELICT and found a bunch of filters to sort the cases into some new categories like: *multiple records, erroneous data, source of data not validated, errors in data, missing personal data,* and *multiple records.* I used several of the pre-defined filters to sort the data in the database. After a considerable wait, I got more than 10,000 target records back, certainly more than I could handle at once, but I started to read through them.

The duplicate and incomplete categories are too difficult to fit into my purpose. Deletes are more interesting. They are the cases where there is a record without a matching person. There is some notation as to the reasons why they were dropped: like illegal aliens who are presumed to have died, disappeared or returned to their homeland. I assume that this sort of information would be imported from INS (Immigration and Naturalization Service) records. Another notation was ITC (International Transport Co.), which I learned later, processed records obtained from private airline companies and the like.

Oy vey, does the average citizen know that this is going on? We should be proud of the thoroughness of the Feds at the expense of privacy. I wondered how much of this is the result of our post 9/11 insecurities?

Then I searched by "death" and "relative" as the filters under "non-credible source," and got 58 hits. 38 were men, only three of which were in their early fifties: Patrick H. Clineholtz, Michael Chen Chi, and Dominique Rodriguez. My genes would not do justice to Michael or Dominique, but Patrick looked interesting, even though he was a gentile, I was prepared to betray my Jewish heritage.

He is recorded to have died at 55, yet there was no validation by the coroner's office. I decided to check this against the 2000 census records, and was satisfied that he was alive and well but without record of whereabouts. He was probably estranged from family and homeless at the time. I checked the census takers location in his case and discovered that it was recorded in San Francisco – another hint that he was homeless when he died.

Just to see what would happen if I changed Patrick's status to alive, DERELICT gave me a big fat error message declaring "you do not have proper authorization to complete this transaction; consult your system analyst." If I am to use Patrick to hide behind, I must find a way to make this modification in the record.

The error message suggesting that I should consult my system analyst gave me some closure for the day. Chip left around five, his usual time to head over to the local watering hole. It is 6:30. I should be heading home. Managing your difficulties rather than letting them manage you is easier said than done.

HERMIT CRAB - Sail A'non

HERMIT CRAB - Sail A'non

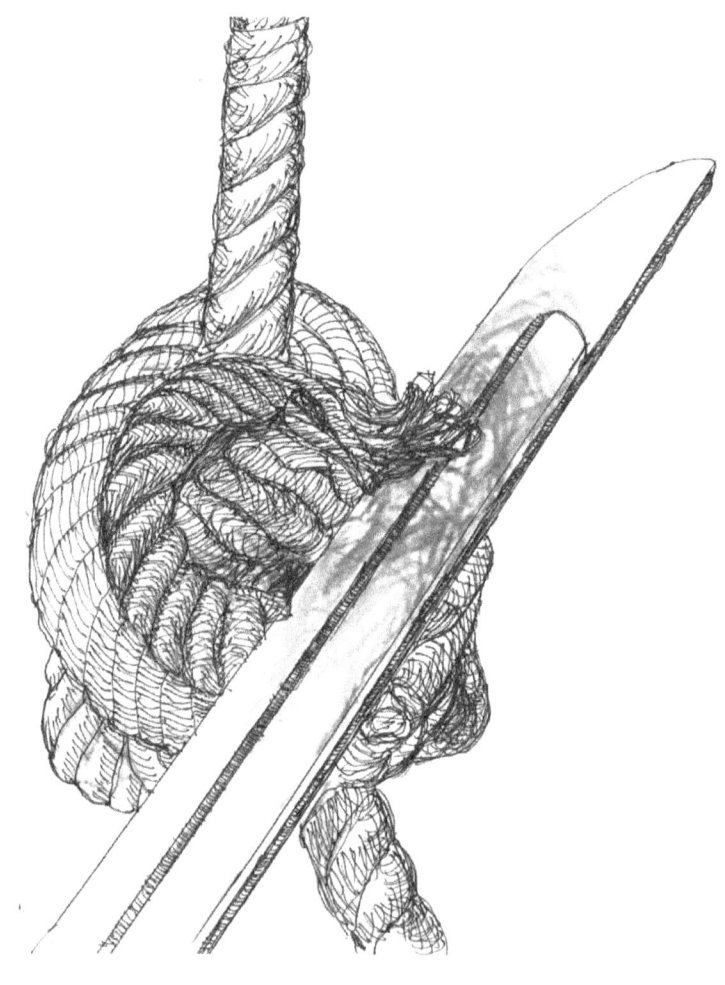

Eight
Deouement

I was self-absorbed throughout the Metro ride. By the time I arrived at the Kiss-N-Ride station it was past seven o'clock; I made it home before eight. Kay was upset. The truce following our Cape May caper was wearing out; she is no longer holding back.

"I hope you ate something wherever you were, because dinner is over and I have no intention to..."

I interrupted her, perhaps for the first time since our prenuptial days.

"You know I was at work, I got absorbed."

"Absorbed is the wrong euphemism, you were lost in the mazes of your brain. You do not get any overtime; the money you're making, after transport, lunch, and those damn books that you buy, is practically gone. You are such a parasite. It is about time you carry your own weight around here, which I have noticed has become considerable lately."

"What are you eating out there for lunch?" Without waiting for an answer Kate continued.

"Y'know those supposedly kosher sandwiches at the mall are made of the same fatty junk from animal factories stuffed with the crap they put inside the burger."

I did not answer and decided to diffuse our fruitless arguments about trivia and reserve my energies to redoubling my effort to finalize my disappearing act. The next day I did another search in DERELICT. Chip was off sick. I will have to wait to see him about added privileges. The same filters as I had used the previous day yielded more entries from records of several other branch offices. This is the time when a lot of data entry is taking place, and I pulled out five suitable cases: Bruce Abercrombie, Melvin Carter, Joseph W. Durkee, Trevor T. Titus, and Ustes Vargas.

These were all good prospects except Ustes. I eliminated him from my short list and added Patrick from yesterday's list. I copied all of their demographics including birth place and last known address. During the lunch break, I called all five registers of vital records at their birth places to orally verify that these records existed at the localities. I explained that I was doing a special project on data validation, at the Bureau. I used the alias Gregg Bell.

I explained that this was just a preliminary query and that they would receive official notification by USPS shortly. This was to discover if the said record was in their database. They promised to get back to me that afternoon and indeed I got some of the calls back the same day.

Lamentably, Patrick was officially dead. His relatives had informed the coroner's and the case was closed. I did not receive a call back for Bruce from Vermont and Joseph from Montana. Trevor was a hit. His records showed that he was alive, while he was a "purge" in our system. Alive locally gone federally, perfect fit for the vacant shell. If I can obtain an identity under the local records, I can reconstruct the Federal records with ease. Paying taxes, obtaining a passport, getting credit cards and bank accounts can create a web of information that would make him a credible character even if the current records have been purged. Perfect; almost too perfect!

I made a handwritten copy of all I found on Trevor and shredded the sheet that contained other names. I am elated and looked around to see if any of the staff had noticed. Trevor's record which I had neatly folded and placed in one of the inner folds of my wallet seemed like a giveaway to anyone who looked at my face. Now that I am at the last stage of my disappearing act; I must remain calm and carry out the rest of my plan with robotic efficiency.

First, I do the paperwork: a postal address, a birth certificate, a SS number, credit cards, library cards, and all of the rest. Next, I will work on appearance to distance myself from Ed as much as possible: new glasses, new clothes, new shoes, some facial hair, a moustache and sideburns may be fitting. This is the fun part.

And, puff I'm gone!

When I reached home, around six o'clock, I found Kay in an unusually chipper mood. This gave me the cover to release my inner joy without being quizzed about it. I simply joined her celebration. She was offered a promotion at AVA. The stats at the office were showing growth especially in areas for which she was responsible – employee relations, retention, and revenues. Similarly, the indications were very positive for the temps placed by her. Feedback from staff and clients were uniformly positive. Kay made sure the staff would give her good marks, by meeting with them ahead of time and unabashedly requested the positive feedback. They complied readily, if not begrudgingly, since they all knew that she was not one to cross. Revenge would be swift for those who did not comply.

In truth, despite these dirty tactics, Kay deserved the credit she got. Now she will be Mr.

Ostergaard's special assistant in charge of all divisions of the firm not just the temp office. She has that flirtatious tone in her voice, which I had not heard in a while. Is she using her femininity to go places? I recalled her phallic reference the other day and had a flashback to an image I had not conjured up since the early days of our marriage: Kay lying on her back with Mr. Ostergaard panting and moaning between her thighs spread wide apart. The human mind is strange. One part of it can conjure up the most unlikely things and the other part can simply say "nah, not possible" and shut the illicit Facebook entry down. If Kay would leave me for another man all problems would be solved. I would reach my goal without becoming the villain in absentia. But who in his right mind would take a real interest in her?

While I am having these thoughts, she is still carrying on about her impending promotion, how she secured it and how she will use it to reach greater heights. She does not rule out becoming the chief officer once Mr. Ostergaard retires. She is full of animated confidence. The words are swirling in the air and hitting my eardrums with percussive tempo. Every now and then her face is becoming contorted, her eyes bulging with excitement.

This reminds me of the insect that I encountered during my Cape May nightmare; and regret the fact that I did not have the resolve to smash it into pieces. The relentless cadence of her voice is picking me up from my seat and carrying me away in the cradle of wave formations all around me. I am no longer able to parse the words and distinguish sentences. I am only hearing a cadence. I feel an urge to lift a great big fly-swatter and slam it, stopping her once and for all.

Bam! I came to my senses, and found my fist had landed on the dining table, having just slammed it by this invisible force inside me. I looked up, Kay was truly perplexed. For a split-second. I was dominating the moment but I knew if I did not find a good explanation, the tables would be turned in an instant. Now, her expression is beginning to turn away from elation...

"That's fantastic!" I yelled. "You worked so hard; I knew all of this would happen someday."

Now, it's her turn to reassess my animated exaltation. "You seem strange today. What's wrong? I've never seen you slam a finger let alone a fist. Are you okay?"

"I'm sorry, there's nothing wrong. I'm sincerely happy for you honeybunch, I just got carried away."

It sounded convincing since I am truly happy today for my own reasons. I realized for the first time that I was almost capable of Hitchcock's

"Rear Window" solution to my problem. What if I could direct the force and momentum of my fist on Kay and squash her like a bug, cut her up and bag her in a trunk?

In this day and age I could not get away with it; too many forensic tools and methods; DNA testing; eye witnesses; you name it. Besides for a man who took 12 years to slam his fist on an imaginary insect on a table, getting to kill and quarter up his wife, would take at least several lifetimes.

The next day at work, I wrote letters to the local vital record's offices of three of the five to try my luck with birth certificates. I came up with imaginative justifications for asking for the certificates. Bruce's letter was from a lawyer working on legal papers for an inheritance case. Joseph was going through a legal adoption application. His step-uncle wanted to include him in his will as his adopted son. Trevor, the chosen one, was going to get his first passport, something I would do as Trevor someday.

I have to have addresses where I can receive replies to my queries. It cannot be a PO Box. So I created a bogus mail box at work. With so many employees and a large turnover rate, no one will notice the appearance or disappearance of a name on a vacant mailbox, in the mailroom. These boxes are constructed from standard 4"x9" mail slots on a 6 high and 25 wide grid, providing 150 individual mail slots. 139 of these were already taken by current employees. I made up an official looking label for Ustes Vargas and pasted it on the 140th 140th slot. In my correspondence with the vital records offices, I used the return address of: Mr. Ustes Vargas Esq., Regional Coordination Office, US Census Bureau, 1227 25th Street Northwest, Washington, DC 20037-1156

Within ten days, I received responses for three of my enquiries. The response from Vermont was negative. In an inheritance case, they required an affidavit or power of attorney before they could issue a copy of the birth certificate. The letter from Montana was even more alarming. They requested Mr. Vargas to submit bar certification and registration information including chapter and member numbers. I started constructing scenarios of being arrested and interrogated by the FBI; for impersonation, obtaining false citizenship records and misuse of federal facilities to perpetuate fraud.

The response to Trevor hit the jackpot and instantly allayed my paranoia. I was holding a copy of his birth certificate in my hands. It happened so suddenly that I put the papers into their envelopes and slowly walked away from the mail room towards my desk as if nothing unusual had happened. This is the turning point of my mission. From here on all I have to do is to follow the routine of my plan and cover my tracks. Compared to obtaining the birth certificate, all else is child's play.

I had deliberately assigned a routine task to the case of Trevor. since he was my top candidate. Compared to issues of adoption and inheritance obtaining a passport should not and did not elevate the bar of scrutiny. Nevertheless, I think that I got lucky. It must be an off day for that someone, trying to clear their desk; simply stuff the envelope with a duplicate birth certificate and mail it to a Census Bureau half way around the country without much thought. Go figure; but I am not complaining. Not one bit!

Next morning, I woke up early and arrived at work in the best mood I could ever remember. I removed the Vargas label from the mailbox. Got a fresh cup of coffee and started going through the steps of my plan. I committed to memory Trevor's Social Security number: 322 48 5059, which I had retrieved from DERELICT for the purposes of Vital Records transactions. This will serve me well enough for the time being.

Now I can conclude my informal report to Saeed: "Usefulness of DERELICT during the Early

Stages of Census Data Entry." The report was all but complete recommending that the approach was sound but had the disadvantage of broadcasting data interactions with sensitive information held at various government agencies. Furthermore, frontend elimination of impaired records was not realistic since most errors were not there to detect. Some data categories were entered at different times and editing and diagnosing of an incomplete record did no one much good. In other words, I confirmed what Saeed had told me, five weeks ago. I know this would appease the old man.

After I turned in my report to Saeed, I did one more thing to bolster my plan. Trevor would have to be purged from the census data in case somehow it is restored into good standing with personal data that belongs to the real Trevor. This can start a chain reaction that would find its way to my, living Trevor. I wanted to hang my shingle on Trevor's shell for good. To do this, I needed access at a systems administrator's level.

I needed the help of the ole bone smuggler: Chip. I decided to treat him for some beer after work on a Friday, his binging day. I convinced him that we should drive out to my old neighborhood and enjoy the authentic ambiance of the Sharp Edge where more the than 100 flavors of Belgian beer are available. I even offered to drive him out and back. This did the trick. At first, I was stunned to learn that he had never been to the Sharp Edge, but it made sense since he is no connoisseur, he is a guzzler.

Sharp Edge is located in a short, one way street connecting two busy residential streets, as a testimony to its blue collar origins. You enter right into the bar area which has the usual, taps, shelves of booze and glasses, flat TV sets and memorabilia of the local sport heroes including football, baseball, and even the Clippers basketball team of the 40's.

In the various rooms to the left of the elongated bar area, which are interconnected by wide passages to accommodate carrying big trays of food, there are large tables for groups. I recognized the table where Kay and I first met. This is an apt revisit for me to nail the coffin on that episode in my life, that is, if I can talk Chip into letting me into DERELICT's secure levels.

As we sat at the bar, I realized that this is going to be a difficult task. I decided that we did not need any distractions and Chip was all too happy to be close to the bartenders. After a few glasses I started with how he had real broad shoulders to carry all the software responsibilities at the office and that he needed quality time to relax. He was visibly pleased.

"That is a real complement coming from a bone smuggler like you. The software part is easy. It's all of those bone smugglers, who want to get around security that pisses me off"

This is going to be a rough climb from his comment to getting around the security system.

"Talking about pissing, the ride all the way here… my bladder is busting."

Chip got up and walked to the back of the bar to take a leak, as I contemplated my strategy to continue the security issue without spooking him. When he returned we talked about how bars have the worst and filthiest bathrooms, what we should order to eat – a perfectly natural transition from bathroom to food – and what's with all this ancient paraphernalia on the walls? In this last topic I found a way to redirect the conversation to the office.

I knew that the boss-woman at our branch, Ms. Spallone, is a descendant of Bobby McDermott, who is recognized by the *Association of Research for Professional Basketball* as one of the top 100 players of the 20th century,. My knowledge of Basketball history was paying off.

"Do you know that our boss woman is Bobby McDermott's daughter." Y'know he was an all-time great who played for the Clippers in the 30s and the 40s."

Chip was in the know. "Get out; then why is she a Spallone and not a McDermott."

Trying to sound convincing I replied "Well I guess maybe she met someone in Italy and fell in love."

"Not that bone smuggler; I don't think she ever got out of Maryland in her entire life."

"I give her more credit than that; she is open-minded. I wanted to do some stuff outside our charge to improve the data robustness and I got her ear. She referred me to a document about census practice at the UK. I still have to track it down…"

"That figures. She must be Irish."

"Let me tell you my idea …"

This did not elicit any reaction from him. He was staring at the portrait of Bobby on the wall. Before he had a chance to digress, I continued.

"If you could filter the data that is entered using DERELICT before it is entered, we could save you and others who do the filtering a lot of time."

I was saying things based on the report I prepared for Saeed, even though the report's conclusions were exactly contrary to the thesis I was dishing out to Chip.

"He looked at me with glazed eyes. He was almost smashed with only four glasses. His liver must be in bad shape, yet there is a hint of incredulity trying to peek through his thick haze.

"Get lost. That would require security checks for all of the data entry bone-smuggling-supers, and changing passwords every week. Not to mention the cat herding I have to do for every fucking bone smuggler in the office when they encounter the slightest problem."

Apparently he was not so smashed after all; he was speaking with great clarity.

"Do you realize how much effort it takes for me to manage my security cleared password for my own account?"

"I hardly ever have to change my password."

"You're a low level bone smuggler. No offense. At my level I have to do it every week; sometimes more frequently. I also have to keep track of it so I don't forget it. With my brain preserved in barley and hops," lifting his glass with a celebratory gesture, "Sometimes even I lose track of it."

"To regain access to a forgotten password of a secure account like mine, is not as easy as sending an email to your mom on Google. You have to do it all on paper. It goes to central for processing. It can take days. Fucking pain! I had to do it only once, but I know the aggravation too well."

His language betrayed his sober mindset. He rarely uses profanities. Perhaps "bone smuggler" is all the release he needs.

"If I hadn't developed this character randomizer-encryptor algorithm, I'd be up shit creek. It's beautiful. It takes 12 characters I enter into it, and it gets randomized automatically before encryption. That's all there's to it. And all of this stuff is based on open source algorithms you can down load from ALGOSOFT on the web."

"How the hell do you keep track of your password of the week then?"

"I was saving it in a file but the problem is if I can't get into my fucking account how can I access that file?"

Now that he was fucking this and fucking that; he seems to have lost the "bone smuggler" lingo all together. I must be right about his lexicographic displacement tendencies.

"So..?"

"So, I rely on the most sophisticated method, ever invented. I write it down."

"In a book?"

"No fucking way you bone smuggler!"

There goes my fancy displacement theory about profanities.

"I write it on my tattoo with a sharpie. Otherwise it washes off in the shower, not that I shower that often, ha, ha."

I already know that without him telling me. In his cubby at the office, there is that unmistakable, faint, but repulsively irresistible odor that suggests that Chip is no great friend of indoor plumbing.

I shivered with excitement realizing that I was inches away from his password of the week tattooed on this filthy human specimen, concealed from my eyes only by a garment or two.

I wondered where his tattoo might be and how I might take a peek at it. What if it is on his ass? This conjured an image of me pulling down his pants and looking at his buttocks, which was terribly disconcerting. It could not be on his ass; that would be hard to reach for him. It must be on his extremities somewhere. Legs are a possibility. Since he is right handed, my best candidate is the left forearm,. I could not help but look at his left arm covered by the sleeve of his leather jacket.

The evening wore on. Chip must have had four more rounds. By the time we decided to leave he was totally drunk and my best buddy. I had to help him to the car where he passed out on the passenger seat, emitting a loud obnoxious nasal groan. I waited a full ten minutes and then decided to do what I would never do under different circumstances: pull up his jacket and shirt sleeves very carefully. It was awkward from where I was sitting with the position of his arm on his lap. But even when I accidentally yanked his arm, his snore preserved its cadence.

Emboldened, I moved his arm onto my lap and stripped it bare. There was no tattoo. As I was getting ready to inspect the other arm, I turned it over and the tattoo of a skull with cross bones and the inscription "bone smuggler" in psychedelic font near a rectangular box was revealed. The box looked like an add-on containing a series of hand written characters in red sharpie. Bingo!

Quick! What do I do now? My brain has slowed down with the alcohol as well. I started looking through my pockets frantically. Found a ballpoint and started copying the 12 character password on the first surface I found, the dashboard did not take. I succeeded to put it on the steering wheels smooth rubbery surface, and then covered up his arm as best as I could.

Chip was too deep in his slumber to mind any of this. Drive home was uncomfortable at best. My blood alcohol must be at DUI levels and I must be very careful not to accidentally rubout the inscription on the steering wheel. I could not afford to make a mistake now. It was late and the traffic was sparse. I did one of my "yes dear, I will get behind that truck and follow" routines.

Deposited Chip at his home. He had processed enough of the alcohol in his blood to be able to get out of the car without help. However, I was not able to stop him from going right on his front stoop. There was no time or inclination on my part to unzip him and pull out his penis with my own hands. Okay stripping his forearm is one thing but this is where I draw the line. What would the neighbors say?

He went all over himself. I took out his keys which mercifully turned out to be in his jacket pocket. I helped him to the nearest sofa in his living room and got out of there as fast as I could. His house was furnished in the typical bachelor geek-squad style: cluttered with piles of computer parts, audiovisual devices, flat screens, processors, tablets, keyboards, and unrecognizable things.

HERMIT CRAB - Sail A'non

HERMIT CRAB - Sail A'non

Nine
Goad

The game is on! I went to work the next day. It was Saturday. There were a couple of data-entry personnel catching up on their work and drawing overtime. I went into my cubby and brought up DERELICT. My access privileges will expire on Monday. I need to do this now. The first try did not work. Not all of the characters I frantically copied onto the steering wheel were legible. I had the option of making the Z a 2 and the O a 0. Or else this password has already been replaced by Chip. I changed the Z, it still did not work. I was afraid that the system would lockdown after the third try. I changed the O and got in!

I found Trevor's record and deleted it. After replying affirmative to a series of questions about "do I really want to do this," the deed was done. I had my empty shell in Trevor T Titus. I realized that I never looked into what the initial "T" stood for. The birth certificate did not have an entry for the middle name. Oh well, it is too late now. I will be Trevor T Titus, whatever that stands for.

What we are as individuals and what society makes us out to be are two very different twines often wrapped into one rope. I am a man of inner consistency, who is often portrayed as a blithering idiot by his wife. She feels entitled to do so through the tenets and practices of matrimony approved by many of our relatives. I deserve to win my freedom as any self-respecting human being, subject to the abuses I endure, would.

The institutions of human societies are too ingrained and powerful: an ornery combination for those who want to change. The only way to be true to yourself is to hide in a cocoon, sneak around social norms, or do the unthinkable. The trouble is, most who engage in these strategies, sooner or later, are considered outcasts or criminals. Ted Kaczynski's or Alexander Berkman's of this world are human testimonials to this principle. I sympathize with a much more kinder-gentler approach. My strategy is an ingenious one compared to the tragedies caused by these characters. I am using a devious but peaceful means to achieve my freewill. The final stage of my task is pretty much mechanical.

On Monday, I took off from work to drive to the Department of Motor Vehicles, at Woodlawn and applied for a new Maryland driver's license. I claimed that my last place of residence was Boston and that my license has been lost. They said that the old record has to be retrieved from *MASS DOT*, the registry of motor vehicles; or I could apply for a new one and take the written and driver's exams anew.

While it required more work and delay of my plan, I opted for the latter in order to start from a clean slate. I returned to Woodlawn a few days later having crammed the driver's exam booklet.

My concentration had been interrupted only when Kay's staff dinner took over hours of my time. Now that she has been promoted to the second highest position in the firm, she was feeling the burden of her increased responsibility as well as the need to flaunt it.

At the DMV, I filled out the required forms, produced my birth certificate and got queued up for the written exam. Passed it and got my learners permit. Scheduled the driver's exam for Friday and decided to visit the eye doctor for the vision exam. It turned out to be a close call. My prescription must be getting old. On Thursday, I stopped at the one hour service for an ophthalmology exam that required a new pair of lenses to be purchased. I picked a frame that has the rectangular look without rims. I also got a set of contacts, the entire time envisioning different looks for Trevor. I used Trevor's name for the paperwork and paid in cash.

This is my first transaction as Trevor which sent chills down my spine.

On Friday, I was back at the DMV a few hours ahead of my appointment. I could not use my car for the exam since my new identity would be encoded with the official record of the car and would lead to my new id as if I had given Kay an invitation to track me down. I staked out the waiting room for a suitable target, and decided on a young man with ordinary outfit.

"I'm sorry to ask for this but I need help taking my driver's exam."

He looked at me with a blank expression, not saying a word.

I continued. "See, I do not have a car. I mean I have one but not at the moment. There was an emergency; my wife had to leave with the family car. She couldn't even drive me here; it is her dad. She had to go directly to the hospital."

More silence.

"So, I figured if I could find someone to loan me a car to drive in the exam, I would be able to get this over with and not have to reschedule. Do you have a car here?"

"Yes, I do." he was not too eager to answer but also did not seem to bulk at the idea which emboldened me to proceed with a proposition.

"I'd be willing to pay you something for it."

His facial expression was less uncomfortable now.

"This will really help me a lot."

Pause.

"I guess it'll be ok. What do I need to do? Oh and when is your exam? I have to be out of here in about an hour."

"If you can say that you drove me here and that it is okay for me to use your car, then that should do it. I'll pay you $100 for the use of the car."

It was a deal. Bruce (that's his name) was even willing to wait an extra half hour to see me through this. To seal the deal I gave him the $100 in advance. Even if he decided not to keep his part of the bargain but keep the $100, I would not mind. He did not seem like the person who would do this. Besides I had more cash on me to try this with others. In the end, it all worked out and I got my license early afternoon on the same day.

Of all the things I owned, this was probably the most important one. Travis Titus with my face besides his name and his address at the census bureau, where I had the forethought to setup a new mailbox for Travis: Mr. Travis Titus, 1227 25th Street Northwest, Washington, DC 20037-1156.

In the event that any correspondence would be sent from the DMV for any official reason, I wanted to be able to receive it.

I drove to work. I wanted to enjoy my new but still secret identity as quietly as a woman who has just discovered that she is pregnant but wants to inform the world in her own good time; savoring the joy privately for as long as possible. The idea that no one out there could know that I am not what I seem to be; that I am being born again, in every possible aspect of societal codification. I am not yet prepared to face the reality of it all, even if in secrecy.

I am in another world; I am euphoric. I walk right into Chip's cubby, which I had been avoiding all week after the tattoo peeking and peeing in pants incident. I was not sure if he was going to remember any of the events of that night, none of which I wanted to revisit.

"What's wrong bone smuggler, did you hit the jackpot?"

I guess my exuberance was plastered all over my face.

"Nothing much; we are ahead of data entry in my sector; just happy to end the week on a high note. Also, I have something planned for Kay, kind of a surprise, so I can't tell you."

"Are you finally gon'na get her drunk?" I felt my face aglow; unwittingly he had hit close to home about last week. He misread my emotion.

"I see, you have some plans for the ole-girl you devil bone smuggler you."

Now I was blushing even more. The thought of getting Kay into the sack was the furthest thought from my mind, but seemed like it could be a memorable parting diversion. I mumbled something about him being dead wrong and that this would be a surprise celebration of her promotion. When I made my way out of there I was reassured that he had no idea that I had breached his security wall.

I went to my desk and started to go through all of my personal belongings that may provide any hint of my clandestine plan. In a strange way, I am enjoying my double identity. I feel in control and powerful. Now, I can become Mr. T at the drop of a hat.

When I arrived home, no bells were ringing or angels singing. It was disappointingly uneventful. Travis had abandoned me in a hurry and Ed took over. Kay was busy with dinner. Jay was doing homework. I went up to the bedroom till dinnertime. Prudence seems to be the best approach. I'd forego glory for the time being if it means avoiding even the smallest risk of slipup. Kay was in an unpleasant mood. I tried to avoid talking to her. Soon I discovered that it had little to do with me.

Jay and I happened to be talking about one of our favorite historical figures, Abigail Adams, when Kay interrupted: "For a change, why don't you stop talking about Abigail and pay attention to the woman of this household?"

"What's wrong honeybunch?"

"Already this promotion is beginning to wear me down. Of all the things I'm doing at the office and the dinners I've been giving at home, Dan [apparently she is on a first name basis with Mr. Ostergaard] is working me down to the bone. Now, I have to go to work tomorrow, maybe even on Sunday."

I knew I had to sound concerned and upset. Jay uttered sincere words of protest. This is the right moment to introduce my plan for the "last supper." I will treat Kay and Jay to a feast before I become Mr. T. Since I can't cook, I will order delivery from our favorite restaurants. This is one of the curve balls I wanted her to think about, when she is trying to figure out my act of disappearance.

"Why don't I treat you to diner tomorrow night?"

"You?" She was almost in shock.

"Honeybunch, I wanted to celebrate your promotion with something nice."

"How on earth do you think you can prepare dinner? I bet you will poison all of us. This will be our last supper."

Is this just coincidence or does she sense something? I always believed that she has a sixth sense about things. It is uncanny how she would know when I bought expensive books, the minute I walked in the door, or was doing something unsavory on the internet, sometimes even before I did them. My denials and protestations would never work, she would see right through me. If she knows something about my plan and has not let me in on it, I should prepare myself for the biggest letdown of my life. As I was reveling in my paranoia, I remembered that the question she asked needed an answer.

"You leave it up to me, I'll manage."

Somehow, this uncharacteristic display of confidence worked. We continued to commiserate for another half-hour. I cleared the table and washed the dishes. It was a quiet evening with each of us retreating into our corners. Kay went to bed early so she could get a head start the next day. Jay got absorbed in reading: he is into Eco; struggling with *Foucault's Pendulum*. I am occupied with the details of my itinerary for tomorrow.

I have a new appearance to construct; a last supper to put together; and abandon life as I know it. Try being Edward Amado someday.

In the morning, I rose with Kay and offered to drive her to work. Since it was Saturday, she was almost expecting it. After dropping her off; I drove to the local strip mall where a national chain was selling discounted brand name merchandise. I got a pair of jeans, a pair of slacks, three Oxfords, a BOSS knock-off leather jacket made in China, sneakers, socks, underwear, two belts, a fedora, cool looking sun glasses, and items of personal care. I do not intend to take with me anything that belongs to Ed. This has to be a total makeover.

For shoes I finally decided to get a pair of imitation alligator boots that I always wanted to have but did not muster up the courage. Since we always did it together, my merchandise shopping was closely scrutinized by Kay. I also got two bags: one durable, for Trevor's stuff and the other a cheap foldaway for Ed's.

I used cash, which I had to draw from the ATM. By the time Kay notices the large withdrawals, it'll be all over. Although we have joint bank accounts and credit cards, she is the minister of finance and she balances the books auditing all statement.

I drove to the Hostel International, downtown to make a prepaid reservation for Trevor for tomorrow night, and left my bags at their *U-Store Self Storage* facility. In this way, I could retrieve them at any time without drawing any attention to myself. There is a bus that links the hostel to the local Dachshund station, almost 24 hours a day.

I had to drive around for nearly three hours to order the food for supper, bought a bouquet of carnations, Kay's favorite, and made it on time to pick her up from the office around 4PM.

"What is going on puts?"

She could not conceal her genuine pleasure at seeing me so attentive to her.

"Are we turning a new leaf?"

All of these comments, unwittingly hitting home, jar me at first; but by now I know to ignore my paranoia and believe them to be just coincidences. So I decided to play along.

"Yes it is a new leaf. We have been together for almost two decades and it is about time we did something about it."

"Like what?"

"Like, like this, nice dinner, flowers, quality time."

I came real close to saying quitting and going our separate ways; but sensibly decided otherwise.

"I do not think you know how much I appreciate what you do for me. You toil at home and at work. You think of what's best for me and

Jay. I just wanted to acknowledge all of that before it is too late…"

"Too late what do you mean?"

Oops, did I slip up?

"I mean we are not getting any younger, I like to stop worrying about the past or trying to second guess the future, and enjoy the present."

"I should call you Ed the Buddha from here on. When did you become so Zen?"

"People are not as static as everyone believes. I think everyone is capable of change and growth."

"That is boloney. People are the same no matter what. Take Kevin," her brother, "He was a complete loser when he was a kid, and he still chisels money from my mom without dad's knowledge. He would be furious if he knew."

"I don't mean that kind of change… or sameness…"

"Do you mean a biological one, like a sex change?"

"No, that is realizing your inner drive. I would not even call it a change. A chameleon is still the same chameleon even if it displays different appearances, or a silkworm that is destined to change is the same creature in a different guise. I mean unplanned but inevitable transformation of the entire thing into a completely different identity, as a result of experience."

"Who are we talking about? Give me an example."

"Like Jay. He was a precautious little terror until four. Then he became this thoughtful, quiet, introvert kid. And yet when he becomes and adult, I wonder what he will become. People do not stay the same. They evolve because of things that happen to them."

"Is that why you are changing; becoming Zen or whatever?"

"No. this is not about me."

"Yes it is, I asked the question about you; don't revise history, your favorite subject, or are you changing that too."

The conversation was getting to be too dicey.

"No I still love history, but honeybunch today is for the two of us, and Jay of course; let's just dwell on these."

I had not declared love to her in at least a decade. Change or not Kay was unable to dismiss these sweet nothings even if she could see palpable changes in me.

Shortly, we arrived home and found Jay in the bathroom with a stack of magazines. When the doorbell rang, he was the one to rush to the door,

"Hey mom there is a man at the door with a lot of packages!"

This was the delivery guy from *Rest-on-Wheels* from whom I had ordered our dinner menu.

I hurried to the door and paid by credit card before Kay could see the bill.

When she came downstairs to see what the commotion was about, not having had a chance to change into her weekend rags, she almost had a conniption.

"I should have guessed you would pull something like this. How could I believe that you would prepare supper by yourself? Talking about change! Can you change into a gourmet chef? Not in your lifetime!"

Without taking a break she added, "How much is all of this going to cost us?'

I tried to put her mind at ease.

"You know I have been doing some overtime at the Bureau for the last month. I am paying for all of this from my extra paycheck."

This softened the blow but still she shifted gears and lectured me on "opportunity cost," a concept remnant from her college days. With the extra money I earned we could have bought a credenza for Jay's room; some pots and pans, a new TV-DVR, or a laptop for her, instead of spending it on things that are expensive and do not keep, like restaurant food.

I decided to ignore this litany and concentrate on other things like setting up the dining room table, pitching minor tasks to Jay, and trying to make it seem all normal. This occasion called for an upgrade from our usual venue in the kitchen. So I pulled out a couple of crystal candle holders from Kay's collection, those I know she has used in the past. In a short time, the table was decked out to both Jay's and my satisfaction. We did not even notice that Kay's tirades ceased altogether.

Kay, having taken a quick shower and relaxed, descended the stairs in her smartest weekend jumpsuit. This is a real mood changer. In spite of the shaky start, the evening turned out as I expected. We had appetizers from *Chez Michelle*, main course from *La Cantina*, and salads and desert from *Casbah*. Wine was purchased by Rest-on-Wheels per my specifications which carried a %25 surcharge. Everything had a delivery fee of %15 which made the total close to $300. This will be my last "gift" to her budget of the month when she receives the credit card invoice.

I felt bad about deceiving her like this. She was genuinely enjoying the evening and grateful for the appreciation with which I have been showering her. What if this is a turning point in our relationship? What if she turns into this sweetest creature that will make my life a pleasure from here on? I looked at her to see if I could penetrate the façade and validate the truth of what I am thinking. Is she this gentle soul trapped in a vindictive cocoon or is she really the witch with a vain indulgence in flattery? She was observing me as well.

"What are you staring at? How many times do I have to wake you up? Sometimes for all the smarts you seem to have, I don't think you have two brain cells to rub together."

There was my answer.

Only if I could throw a bucket of water on her and watch her melt into her shoes. The game is on; I am going to become Mr. T after the stroke of midnight, tomorrow.

The rest of the evening was routine. Kay thanked Jay and I for a lovely evening and retired to her embroidery before bed. Jay and I cleaned the table, packed the fridge with the leftovers, and filled the dishwasher. We sat at in the living room for a while. This is unusual but so is the entire evening. We started discussing *Foucault* and how he collapsed time: centuries into years, years into months, months into days and days into minutes.

He was impressed with the references to the Middle Ages and things we think we know about, while realizing the possibility of interpretations we never imagine. Duality and duplicity of things that is most familiar to us being scary. I told him about the *Island of the Day Before* as a superb example of this; how a man and his dual opposite are juxtaposed in a geographic duality of time, the day before and after staring each other in the face.

"When you finish *Foucault* you should read the *Island*." "I'll put it in your room tomorrow."

"Ok, well I'm not done with *Foucault* yet. You can give it to me later."

Then he looked at me as if he understood that I was not going to be around for long. I think he has his mom's sixth sense.

"Dad, are you going somewhere?"

I did not panic, nor tried to conceal. "I might; then I might not; it's life."

I am beginning to believe that the Zen approach offers a good out for these situations. You can be ambiguous just so that you skirt around an out-and-out lie as well as spill the beans all together.

"I think the world of you dad. What you did for mom tonight was great."

He looked at me with puppy dog eyes and came over to give me a hug. This is a real bear hug. I have not had one of these – discounting the ones I get from aunts – since the ones I used to get from mom when I got a licking from the street bully named Hugo. This is a very rare occasion indeed for Jay's age and for this household. Instinctively, I whispered mazel tov under my breath. It was just loud enough for him to hear. I was tearing up when he suddenly pulled back and said "goodnight" without looking at me and ran up the stairs to his room.

I sat there for at least another hour just hating myself for what I am about to do.

Sunday was uneventful, even though there was inner turmoil and torment for me. I drove Kay to work and brought Jay along to spend a few hours alone time with him at the National Aquarium, one of our favorite attractions in town. It was a great diversion for me and him. Jay had shown such delight to see me this morning that I think his previous night's anxiety about me seems to have evaporated. We spent most of our time with the reptiles and poisonous creatures of the sea. A good portion of this was in the tunnel under the sting ray pool.

Neither of us liked the seal show but just to kill time we stopped at the amphitheater until Kay called to be picked up. We drove home in relative calm. I am dealing with my sadness.

This is probably the very last time I would enjoy Jay's company. Next time I spend time with him, if I ever do, he may be an adult.

On the way home, Jay dozed off in the back seat. Sunday lethargy has set in. Kay was bushed from nonstop work, which shut even her up. We ate leftovers and gathered around 60 Minutes on TV. It showed reruns on account of the approach of the Fall schedule. After the usual kitchen, homework, house cleaning chores, we all retired around 10PM.

Two more hours till D-day!

I could not go to sleep for hours. I was full of anxiety, remorse, fear, self-loathing, and confusion. I decided to let things happen. I would just sleep over it. I revisited my plan and connected the dots; all the work I did to create each dot, the life I have been planning for myself for years now, and the woman snoring in the double bed near me.

A set of new emotions began to overtake me: excitement, hope, freedom, love, levity, peace. Before I knew it I dosed off. I woke up in a panic, it was still dark. I snuck out of bed; went to the bathroom. It was 3:30. There is still time if I act now. I am not a compulsive man but there is no time to think things over. When your boat is pulling anchors, you have to be on it.

I went to my closet. Kay was still snoring. Took my pajamas off; grabbed a pair of slacks, belt, long sleeve shirt, some socks, and went down stairs. I dressed quickly; put on the windbreaker that I had stuffed with my wallet and vital documents, into the bag, the night before. I walked out into the cool spring night with an eerie sense that I am being watched.

I do not dare look back at Jay's bedroom window.

HERMIT CRAB - Sail A'non

HERMIT CRAB - Sail A'non

Ten
Exodus

I walked to the Silver Spring Metro Station on East-West Highway – who in his right mind sets up a name like this? I decided to walk along Georgia Avenue bidding farewell to my favorite car rental palace, next to our bank, and the arts and craft store to which Kay transfers money from next door on a regular basis.

I am taking in all that I can see in the hazy light of this cool, dusk morning hour. I will probably never perceive exactly these same sights, smells and sounds, for the rest of my life.

I stopped at the bank to withdraw the maximum amount allowed for the day. I consider myself entitled to a little bit of our joint capital to start my next life. This is my third withdrawal since Friday. I accumulated a little over two grand.

I am early for the five o'clock train. I bought a copy of the *Sun* to take my mind off of the anxiety of my mission, The *Jewish Times* has filed for bankruptcy; the mayor is slashing the budget; a little girl has disappeared; and South Baltimore 911 crime tapes have been released.

On the bright side, "Baltimore" is mentioned on the first line of Kitty Kelley's unofficial biography of Oprah; a council woman recalls how she created a prom dress from "vintage castoffs;" and several fashion stores are offering cheap deals. This is the same nonsense to which we have been subjected for the last three decades; yet it is reassuring at this moment to note that the world has not stopped just because I'm changing trains. I will not miss any of this; in fact, I can guarantee that wherever I end up, this sort of crap will still be all around.

The train is practically empty with the exception of some poor souls who have to be at work by six, or have to catch an early plane, train or bus – like me. I get off at the Union Station and hop on MARC to Shot Tower Station, downtown Baltimore, which is a short walk to the Hostel International on Mulberry, where I am registered.

I go directly to the U-Store facility and retrieve my luggage; then check in; go up to my room; change into my new outfit. The slacks are a little too long. I fold the hems up and crease them with a damp towel. This will do for now. It is better that they are not too short, which would be a lot harder to fix.

I do not have a moment to waste. Kay and Jay will wake up shortly. Emotionally, I want to be on that bus before anyone is aware of my absence. I check out of the hostel. It is a 15 minute walk to the Goodwill on Redwood. I drop my old belongings into the overnight bin; then walk a few blocks back to Saratoga and catch the municipal bus #27 to the Dachshund Bus station. I am there at 7:15. Kay and Jay must be up by now wondering where I am. That is also what I am trying to figure out.

The earliest bus to a major Westward destination is the 7:45 to Chicago. I buy the ticket without much hesitation. This is the decision I had deliberately left out of my plan. I know I have to put some distance, psychological and otherwise, between myself and Kay. Therefore, the East coast is out. I do not want to go South, where the climate is homogeneous and uncomfortable for my constitution. Besides, there is the stigma of ending up at a retirement venue, unless you end up in New Orleans – now that's a thought! If it weren't for the devastation of Katrina, it would be a real contender. The Pacific, on the other hand, has plenty of options and diversity of people and places, up and down the coast. I will head west, and settle down where the spirit compels me to do so.

Now, I am officially Trevor T Titus. Everything worth having in life has its price. I paid the price by losing everything I had to gain my freedom. My heart aches every time I think about Jay and the hug he gave me last night; I also left a sizable collection of excellent books behind. Not much else that I abandoned has any value for me.

The walk along Georgia Avenue this morning brought back many memories of my teen years in Silver Spring that are becoming more distant with each passing minute. I engaged in lying, cheating, stealing, misrepresenting, and betraying my character in order to get to this point. My only consolation is that none of that is with me any longer. It is all in the past. They belong to Ed not Travis. I realize that this is yet another deception – in fact it is the mother of all deceptions – but I assure myself that it is the final one. Trevor is starting with a clean slate; and it will stay that way, so help me God.

Those whose time has come for punishment by gods end up boarding an intercity bus for one reason or another. I was near the front of the line with very little luggage, so ended up seating myself in the middle along a window at the driver's side of the bus. I could not shake the feeling that Kay's face with the brown ooze spewing from her mouth will materialize anytime now, just outside of my window.

A heavy set, smelly, guy in an orange jump suit accompanied by a US marshal is seated in the window seat across the aisle from me. I never knew that this was possible. Here he was, handcuffed and staring at me.

The bus filled out quickly. The driver approached me and asked if I would like to move to another seat since the prisoner's seat was reserved for security reasons and another marshal would sit across the aisle from him. I still must be in purgatory. Reluctantly I complied. The only reasonable seat left was beside a diminutive man about my age, who seemed to be minding his own business.

"May I? I've been asked to move here [gesturing to the driver behind me]. I mean... not here... but out of my seat..."

You can take the man out of Ed Amado, but you can't take Ed Amado out of the man.

"It's fine man. The seat is yours. It does not even belong to me to give it away. Ha, ha."

He spoke with a slight German accent. I thanked sheepishly and settled in.

"Hi I'm E... I mean Travis."

"You don't know who you are?"

"No it's not that I've had a hard day... I mean morning; night and morning/"

"You are lost my little lamb. Zoltan. Zoltan Zumthor. That's usually a mouthful for most, so they call me Gerhard. That's my middle and starter-name for new acquaintances. Pleased to meet you E-Travis."

Great start Travis, you bumbling moron!

"Pleased to meet you too... Gerhard"

Change the subject, fast!

"Where are you heading?"

Idiot! Chicago of course; stop inching along on moron-gear.

"I mean are you heading all the way to Chicago?"

"*A good traveler has no fixed plans, and is not intent on arriving.* Relax my man. Whatever trouble you're running from, it's ok; Zumthor will take care of you."

Out of the pan into the fire! I think I prefer sitting by the US Marshal, but it is too late now. I did not even bother to deny that I was indeed running away. It probably would be no use. He would see right through it. Who the hell would call their child Zoltan Gerhard Zumthor anyhow? If I have my facts right probably a Swiss mother who believes in goodness, strength and Zumthor, whatever that means.

So, I tried to find out: "Are you Swiss? I mean by birth... Of course..."

"Of course ... I'm glad you caught yourself this time. I am American, as American as the next guy, but yes I was born at a Canton on the Alps, the name of which I do not care to remember any more, many years ago, before I ran away too."

He continued, "I consider myself a citizen not a national of any country. It only leads to mischief. *When a nation is filled with strife, then do patriots flourish!*"

This last phrase he uttered with an air of an orator sounds familiar but I cannot place it.

I replied, "I am Jewish."

I am still unsettled and trying so hard to make up for each *faux pas* that I top it with even bigger ones.

"That's ok man, you could do much worse. I'm kidding. I do not give a flying fuck about organized religion. You do what you dig, man. I... I prefer disorganized religion myself."

"What is that?" Relief! Ask questions; pass the buck. Travis, you're not Ed any more, try and relax god damn it!

Gerhard explained, "Disorganized religion has no tenets, edicts, encyclicals, fatwas, or rules to follow. *It is better to do one's own duty, however defective it may be, than to follow the duty of another, however well one may perform it. He who does his duty as his own nature reveals it, never sins.*"

I swear to god he is not making this stuff up. I know it's from some source I should know. He is full of shit. He is a charlatan, a marionette; but who is pulling his strings.

The bus had taken off a while ago; and I noticed only now. I am beginning to relax a bit. I tried to cool down the conversation and focus on letting Travis in. I tried to just sit there without a word; but Gerhard was on a roll.

"I am a man of the world. I take it as it comes and I enjoy the ride. You can hardly beat that with a stick even if you wanted to. *Of all that is good, sublimity is supreme. Succeeding is the coming together of all that is beautiful. Furtherance is the agreement of all that is just. Perseverance is the foundation of all actions.*"

He is stark raving mad. This went on for a while. Since I had had so little sleep the night before, I must have dozed off. I woke up with Gerhard tugging at my arm.

"Wake up! It is joint break; we're in Altoona, man."

I got up and let him pass. Tried to go back to sleep but the entire bus was exiting. I had to pee. I dragged Travis out of the door and into the sanitary facilities that were all but. As I was doing my best John Wayne and Madame Butterfly strut towards the bus – the lack of sleep always hits hard where it counts– Gerhard sequestered me between the bus and his persistence. He offered me a puff from his joint. I looked around and saw one of the US marshals looking in our direction. How do I get rid of this asshole? I declined and pushed my way past him into my miserable seat.

This went on for another nine hours until we reached Cleveland. When I bought my ticket with an impulse, I did not bother to check the arrival time or if I did I must have confused AM with PM. We still had another 10 hours before the suburbs of Chicago. This is going to be hell. My only conciliation is that if anyone is looking for me they will never find me in this insane asylum on wheels.

This is as surreal as it gets. You step into this moving, metallic, oblong object and the order of life is completely altered. People fart, piss in plastic containers, smell real bad, devour stuff that rats in NY would thumb their whiskers at, transport convicts, smoke pot, and make everyone around you real nervous. Finally we reached the outskirts of Chicago. Gerhard was still on a roll. This time he had engaged the kid sitting behind him, lecturing on the virtue of diligence.

"Ant on the move does more than a dozing ox."

Despite my aversion to this guy, he comes up with stuff that is either brilliant or plagiarized from a very good source. In either case I have to give him some credit. When we arrived at the central bus depot, I gathered my things and said a quick bye to him, but before I could move on he grabbed my arm.

"I know you're in trouble my good friend E...Travis. So listen to me carefully: *When virtue is lost, benevolence appears, when benevolence is lost right conduct appears, when right conduct is lost, expediance appears. Expediency is the mere shadow of right and truth; it is the beginning of disorder."*

As I walked away from the bus depot, having relieved my proximity anxiety to Baltimore and relatively rested, my brain cleared up: Lao Tzu, he is quoting Lao Tzu! Son of a bitch, I liked my mad companion a smidgen more.

I was lucky enough to find a single at the Hosteling International right across from the Grant Park, downtown. A much needed shower and a catnap restored me back to normalcy. I woke up rehearsing my new name and identity in my head. It seems to have turned into a mental exercise. If I'm to avoid future screw ups, I need to turn this into a habit.

I took a stroll at Grant Park. I had just enough time to take in the lobby of the Art Institute Museum, the Millennium Park, before finding a Mexican restaurant for some enchiladas. Harold Washington, one of my favorite public libraries, happens to be a stone's throw from the hostel. I had time to do some research on San Francisco, Oregon and Seattle, where the seasons are more to my liking. There are a lot of small towns around San Francisco, which can help me hide in the quiet privacy of a small "pond." But there is always the risk of becoming a big fish that attracts attention. In my state of uncertainty, the idea of being a tiny fish in a large pond is probably the best.

Oregon is the most "bucolic" of the three. It is the sort of place I would have liked to be born into. Seattle on the other hand seems to have all of the features I am looking for. It is large but not too large; liberal but not too liberal; diverse and homogeneous at the same time; and has four seasons.

I cannot stand another bus ride, this time even longer, across the continent. I searched airline deals on one of the desktops at the library. Found a cheap flight for the day after. Made a reservation and planned to purchase the ticket at the airline agency. I still do not have credit cards for Travis, so all transactions will have to be in cash, which often meets with curious smiles or puzzlement.

Every now and then, I can't help but loan my mind to Jay and our parting. Kay is completely out of sight, out of mind, except during my paranoia spells which are happening less often. The farther I move away from the East Coast, the less likely am

I to look over my shoulder. My plan has been so carefully designed and executed that unless one looks at all surveillance cameras in the entire nation, there is no way of tracking Ed down. Travis, on the other hand, is a stranger to Kay, both on paper and in the flesh.

I spent a peaceful night in my room, which has its own bathroom and is quite clean for a hostel. I could not part from my copies of Joyce and Melville, so I have them in my backpack with me. I read myself to sleep.

The next morning I woke up, once again, rehearsing my new identity in my head. Found a bagel shop on the way to the airline agency. My payment method is clearly unusual for the young lady at the airline bureau. She examined my id with extra care and probably figured that I did not fit the standard profile of a terrorist.

I felt the need to explain,

"I lost my credit cards. I believe I left them at the airport bathroom. I went back but they were gone. Someone must have found them. Fortunately, I had my bankcard and cash still on me."

She explained, "You can't be careful enough. You should notify the credit card companies or you will be looking at very large charges."

I confirmed, "Yeah, I believe they cover it after a deductible."

Now, I have an entire day to kill – no, to enjoy! – in Chicago! I high tailed it to the Art Institute, one of my favorite museums. As I approached it, I spotted the man who was fashioning a body bill board, walking back and forth in front of the cascading steps of the main entrance. I hope this is not some sort of a labor strike or something. As I came closer I could read the text on his back:

"If you have to move your bowels, do it."

"If you feel tired, lie down and sleep."

As I got closer he turned around and started walking towards me. Now I could read the beginning of his message:

"If you are hungry, eat."

"If you have to pass water, take a leak."

"*over* ⇨"

As he passed me he handed me a pamphlet. It is crudely done on an old copy machine, probably dating back to the days when copying was called Xeroxing, and copies were hand collated. It is simply titled "Lao Tzu. "

What are the chances? Either all coo-coos are into Lao Tzu, or this is an omen. My curiosity is awakened. I folded the pamphlet; stuffed in my back pocket; and promptly shifted my attention to the museum. The new modern addition to the art gallery by Renzo Piano is impressive. Clean, white, with glorious natural light from above, covered with these new fanged crinkled louvers spanning from one end of the atrium space to the other. I spent a good bit of time looking at the spaces and the permanent collection.

The show's in the new wing of the museum. Architecturally speaking there is nothing in this section to write home about. I noticed that since the immersive experience with Zumthor, Travis has been absorbed in clichés. Have to get him out of this unpleasant habit.

I left the museum for a stroll in the Loop. I caught lunch at the same chain Mexican semi-fast-food restaurant. I am not a fan of shopping, yet my new found freedom seems to have lifted my inhibitions. I feel cloaked in this urge to try anything that comes along. So I found myself in Neiman Marcus, staring mindlessly at jewelry and perfumes.

"May I help you with anything?"

"No, thanks; just browsing"

"Maybe something for the missus?" He is a clean cut young man with a pleasant smile, slight slur of the "s" and a gay intonation in his words.

"No, not for the missus; I'm just window shopping."

"That's quite alright sir, let me know if I can be of any assistance. We have some excellent bargains in the *Allure* line; for men of course."

I said "No thanks" once more and moved on.

His remarks followed me for a few more seconds. "That's quite alright. If you change your mind please look for me; my name is Ronnie."

And with these words he moved on to another approaching customer. I should get myself to the men's department before, once again, Travis makes a fool of himself.

I always wanted to buy a really cool tie that would somehow distinguish me in an unusual way: like a really skinny leather one to match my faux-leather jacket. I found a very small collection of conventional colors, brown, beige, black, and a knit pattern of three colors. I spent almost a fortune on the knit tine. There is a real thin line between new found freedoms and silly overindulgence. I put the tie on my golf shirt even though the collar was a bit wobbly for a tie, especially a leather one that is knit. I just wanted to test my newfound fashion sense.

I strolled through the streets of downtown Chicago for hours thinking about my emancipation as well as predicament. Until I get my bearings re-positioned I still feel that Travis is in limbo. How will he realize his hopes and aspirations? I have to try harder to get Zumthor-isms out of my mind. Is Travis going to have a steady job; a home; a dog; a wife; children; and a library that would be the envy of George?

Absorbed in these thoughts I came upon a park bench; took my Lau Tzu pamphlet and started looking for a gem that may help me think through all of this. And there were a lot of them that I could apply to Travis. I focused on: *"All difficult things have their origin in that which is easy and great things in that which is small"*

I have to find the *small* in Travis; and the *easy* for setting up his life. He is what I make him to be. But this must be within the scope of Edward's ethos. This is not a randomized process of mixing up some genes dictated by chance meetings in bars or the exigencies surrounding the upstream swim of sperms. This must be intentional design – and not what they mean by "intelligent design." I have to *create* in the true sense of that word; make something from nothing. I see myself as the hand holding the compass in William Blake's depiction of how the universe was created, except that I have to train my measuring device on Travis, a much simpler subject matter, than that of God.

Since my flight to Seattle is early in the morning, I walked into a bar near the hostel to catch an early supper. It is dark and atmospheric. I sat at a barstool and began to look at the menu. I started with some Amsteel beer, which made me recall one of the more memorable visits to the Sharp Edge. Despite my inner angst, there was no anticipation in this bit of nostalgia. Travis and the change of venue are cleansing the cathartic aspects of my life like so many *Scrubbing Bubbles* gliding inside a bathroom bowl. While I was trying to pick out the menu item from among things like Bowl's Over, South of the Border, Pie Hole Pizzas, Heart Attack Tater Tot Casserole and just as I was settling on some Machos Nachos; I heard a familiar voice calling out to me.

"Imagine seeing you here?"

In the darkness of the bar, I could not place the face immediately, but the voice was unmistakably that of the young man at Neiman Marcus, which curiously made me happy. He is the first acquaintance I've made.

"Oh hi!"

"Remember, Ronny from Neiman Marcus?"

"Sure I do, what a coincidence, twice in the same day."

"Lovely coincidence," with these words he moved on towards a table where some of his friends must be seated, since they gave him an enthusiastic greeting.

I looked around and realized that this is a gay bar. It was not just a coincidence that Ronny walked in; the bar is just around the corner from

Neiman Marcus. I ordered my Machos Nachos and started watching the nightly news on the TV screen mounted on the wall across from the bar. By the time I was done eating Ronny paid me another visit. He was the life of the party. Dressed in a smart white plaid jacket, light orange shirt, and smart fitted light blue pants made his choreography of expressive motions visible from across the room.

Pointing to my tie: "I like it. I'm glad your shopping went well."

"Oh yeah, I always wanted to have one but my wife never approved."

"I thought there was no missus."

Quick, think of a good line Travis, don't blow this one!

"Not any longer," a curt and fuzzy answer.

"No, it's not like that…" More cover commentary by Travis.

Don't blow it; change the subject. While I was thinking, Ronnie did it for me.

"So, what are you doing in Chicago? You don't look like you're from around here."

"I'm just passing through. I am heading in the direction of Seattle."

"Oh really? I have a twin sibling in Seattle: Robin; she is the love of my life. Do you live there? You must meet her." He went into an elaborate praise of her and how he misses her.

A little later the "open bar cabaret hour" was announced and with accompaniment of recorded music some of the customers stepped up, onto the bar, and began showing their moves. This was certainly entertaining. I had never seen anything as expressive as this, even in the Karaoke Night I once witnessed, quite by accident, at a suburban bar at Baltimore frequented by Koreans. Ronny held my shoulder tenderly and came close to my ear to make sure I would hear him with the music blasting not too far from us,

"Listen, you must stay to see me strut next,"

I replied, "I have an early flight tomorrow; I have to go in a little bit."

"Ok, well here," he grabbed a piece of paper from the bartender and scribbled something on it.

"This is Robin. She works at the Central YMCA. When you get to Seattle, give her a call and my love, too. Bon voyage!"

With that he walked over to the end of the bar where there were steps and climbed up. He is really good. His jacket is off and you can follow the elegant motions of his upper body in perfect rhythm with the music. He must have studied dance. Gradually the motions became centered on his pelvic and groin area to cheers from the direction of his friends, which only helped amplify his evocative motions. Suddenly, I felt out of place and uneasy. So far as I know, I am not gay, so what am I doing here? Curiosity? Perhaps. I think I satisfied it if that is all there is. The thought of belonging here is an alien idea – "not that there is anything wrong with that," in Larry David's inimitable words. Larry provides the ultimate Jewish reinterpretation of life. I believe all Jews who want to belong in today's world should stop reading the Torah and watch the entire reruns of "Curb Your Enthusiasm." I am learning new things about Travis: he is blasphemous.

I left the bar, while Ronny was still on "the stage." I waved when he spotted me. He tossed me a kiss. Travis has made a friend on the third day of his life, albeit a brief one. Still, it feels good.

I arrived in Seattle early in the morning. With the time difference it was as if no time had elapsed, but I was tired from the early morning rise in Chicago and the long flight. Since I am running out of money, I wanted to find a cheap place to stay. I went to the information booth looking for a hostel. The most reasonable and well located one was the YMCA.

I pulled out the piece of paper Ronnie had given me the night before. It said: Robin, YMCA, 909 4th Av, 206 382-5010. I boarded the Metro Bus service to downtown and headed straight to the Y. I asked for Robin. She was busy running a fitness class for older folks. I decided to wait for her to finish the class. I got some free coffee from the courtesy table, and some nachos from the vending machine to quiet my growling stomach. Airline food is not what it used to be – in fact it certainly is what turned into airline food, as we know it.

Robin is great looking; perhaps the best one whose acquaintance I've made so far. She is fit, trim, beautiful face, red head, tucked up nose with proportional cheekbones, full lips and a killer smile. I think I am already in love. The way she moves reminds me of Ronny. I pull myself together and start explaining myself as succinctly as possible in order to get quickly passed that "what does this guy want?" look on her face.

"Hi, I'm Travis. I brought greetings from Ronny. In fact he sent his love."

This must be the secret password. Her smile returned. "Hi Travis; good to meet you; how's Ronny?"

"He's great. He was having a great time the last time I saw him, which was last night. He made sure that I should see you and pass on his greetings. I must also confess that I have an ulterior motive. I just stepped off of a United flight and am also looking for a place to stay for a few nights. I thought the Y may be a good place to start looking."

"Oh, hey that's no problem. Any friend of Ronny's a friend of the Y. If you were a woman I could set you up in our King Court residence but alas, no such luck!"

I can see the bubbly personality of Ronny in her, too. "If you're looking for a hostel type accommodation, I recommend the City Hostel. It is clean reasonable and I know someone there who can help."

She made a few calls and talked to someone for five minutes, mostly about other things. "Ok you're set. You should see Mark at the main desk. They have shared 4-bed-rooms with shared baths for $55 including tax. He'll put you in a room by yourself; at least initially you'll have some privacy."

"Sounds great, thanks Robin,"

She was already waving good bye and moving on to something else." Hey, no sweat; let me know how it turns out. Keep in touch."

Then she suddenly stopped on her tracks.

"I never asked, how you got to know Ronny" Detecting my hesitation, she turned around and left "Ok, I get it, Bye!"

She was gone. I can see how this one egg split in the womb and produced replicas that have the same behavioral imprints that supersede gender, environment, and all kinds of external influence. I am impressed by the invariants of the human condition in spite of the volatile sides of our nature to which Travis sets a good example – one that is not yet as powerful as behavioral congruity. I just witnessed, but one that is convincing even in its embryonic form. I feel the impatient exuberance of a mother, or even a creator of minor beings, watching her masterwork flourish before her eyes. I am full of vivre this morning, thanks to Robin, Ronny and of course Travis.

For a few weeks, until I find a job to establish myself financially and before I would have to resort to soup kitchens and homeless shelters, the City Hostel will serve me well enough.

HERMIT CRAB - Sail A'non

Eleven
Bliss

At the end of my first month in Seattle, I secured a position at Barnes and Noble, which was my first and last stop in my job search. My resume made me a shoe in for the Assistant Floor Manager position at the downtown branch. Thus, I started looking for an apartment. The transit population of the City Hostel was not the best incubator for nurturing Travis' toddler-size personality. He had no social life. So he found an excuse to see Robin a few times but she turned out to be super busy and difficult to rope in. Her energy is like a fireball that defies containment; besides, in action, she is such a beauty to watch that it extinguished any desire Travis had to slow her down.

Encounters are brief at best. She asks Travis how things are. They reminisce about Ronny in passing. She helps with Travis' daily queries, but she disappears as quickly as she appears. There is no room in these interactions for getting personal or intimate. There does not seem to be any desire on her part to go beyond a casual friendship, yet she is our entire lifeline. I am clinging to this idea in my head as if Travis' life depends on it.

I have to stop thinking of Travis in the third person. This can turn into a serious case of split personality.

In reality, there is another woman in my life; the kind I want to avoid. She is Kathy, my boss. She reminds me of Kay in many respects, not counting the fact that she is my boss. She is a small woman full of nervous emissions, with no resemblance to Robin's positive energy. When she speaks, and that seems to be the steady state for her, these little balls of white foam collect at the corners of her ultra-thin lips; and grow and shrink as a function of the intensity of her oratory. Since I've never seen her wipe these tiny balls of air trapped in saliva, I assume she does not seem to be aware of this unusual saliva phenomenon or she just does not care. I recall some words of wisdom from Lao Tzu –I guess I developed a habit of reading that accidental acquaintance: *"He who is contented is rich."*

Kathy seems content with her condition. It is others, such as I, who get distracted. Every now and again I catch myself paying absolutely no attention to her words and slide into a trans just watching the saliva balls roll over so gradually in their sockets and gather firmament and energy as she talks incessantly about one B&N procedure or another. Once or twice, I almost got into trouble with her when it became clear that I was so distracted watching them that I did not follow her instructions.

Lao Tzu also says *"He who knows himself is enlightened."* Is it better to be rich or enlightened? I take the latter. Furthermore, *"He who controls others may be powerful, but he who has mastered himself is mightier still."* Powerful versus even mightier; there, take that Kathy!

She is not all that bad as a boss: demanding but fair. Nothing I could not handle within a professional relationship which is what she expects and I am happy to provide. She seems to be satisfied with my performance and this job is the core of my life as Travis. Based on my new motto in life, I am keeping things as "easy and small" as possible.

Walk before running, crawl before walking, and get your legs under you before crawling. Get a job, keep a job, and grow in the job. Start reading, get a book collection, and build a library. Rent an apartment, buy a car, and buy a house. Love a woman, marry a woman, have kids. Eat, piss, shit, and sleep. Simple, basic, and at the core of human existence: keep it simple and existential; that is what "easy and small" means.

On the anniversary of the second month of my emancipation, September 15 to be precise, I am celebrating the accomplishment of the first tier of my philosophy of easy and small: I have a nice apartment, a satisfactory job, have started a modest book collection, am in love with Robin – even though she seems oblivious – and to boot: I can eat, piss, shit (hemorrhoids permitting) and sleep. Mazel tov!

My big break with Robin came when Kathy invited the staff for a cookout at her backyard. She knew that putting a personal face on things even within the bounds of duty, obligation, and work makes for a happier staff and a happier boss-woman. She mentioned something about inviting spouses, partners, significant others. After some soul searching and creative interpretation of what a significant other might mean I decided Robin was certainly significant enough to qualify for my "other." This is the litmus test for us. I'll find out if she is interested or not, once and for all. Anticipating the worst, I went to see her with the excuse of finding out if she knew where I could get good second hand books in Seattle, aiming at two birds with one stone.

"I've been trying to get a library together and don't know the best places to look."

"I am not a big reader – I get easily distracted – but even I know about the *Half Price* at the university district. That's where you should go. You know what; let's look at the internet, that's the best way to find out."

Knowing how web savvy I am, Robin's suggestion exposed my pretext for what it is. No matter, as we huddled near the desktop in the office, the close proximity to her body, the fresh shampoo smell of her hair, anticipation of what I am about to ask her, and my heart beating uncontrollably, while trying to sound casual, I got all cramped up. Saliva accumulating in my throat bloated out my voice chords beyond their normal function and I was only able to utter a grunt:

"Ugh!"

I cleared my throat "Hmm, hem!".

"Are you ok?"

Robin was staring at my crimson face.

"Oh yea, I'm ok. I just wanted to ask you if you would like to go to a barbeque with me this weekend."

There it's done.

"What's the occasion?"

I tried to explain, "Well, my boss... Well it's really my intent to celebrate the second month anniversary of being in Seattle. In truth I am piggybacking on a staff cookout at Kathy's."

"Sure, why not; when is it?"

Whew! This is a real milestone. She does not seem to be attached, and she accepted my invitation without thinking. Even if it is for the sake of pity, I'll take it gladly. I am not as shabby looking as Ed. I dress smart, as smart as my salary allows. A few weeks ago, I started working out, courtesy of Robin. She hooked me up with one of the YMCA-retired stationary bikes for $100. I spin for at least 30 minutes each morning and already see the benefit of that on my stamina. I guess she could do worse.

When Saturday came along, I felt uncomfortable with the idea of dating. I have been out of practice for decades now. I took the bus to her home and we drove to Kath's in her car.

The barbeque was a casual affair and nothing much happened, not even to match the innocent closeness provided by the hair aroma moment at the Y. As I expected, Robin was the life of the party. She made some friends mostly with young available men, which should have made me feel jealous. Instead, I felt like withdrawing into my shell; learning to know my place among these eligible rivals.

What helps is the sense that Robin while obviously enjoying the attention she gets is not overtly flirtatious as Kay would have been. She is not using her femininity; she is like one of the boys. For the first time, observing her outside of the Y, where athleticism is everyone's overt posture, I noticed something Tom-boyishly sexual about her.

Several times she reached out to me as well. We had pleasant conversation about the people she met, Kathy, her family of five – including two daughters, a son and a husband who is absent at the moment – and how neither of us would be able to survive in this kind of suburban isolation even if we could afford this gorgeous ranch house.

I blurted out one of my Lao Tzu gems: *"When you are content to be simply yourself and don't compare or compete, everybody will respect you."*

"Trev" [She has assigned me a nickname already and I do not dare say that I hate it for fear that I may hurt her feelings]. "This is what is so refreshing about you. You look like a regular guy and speak like a genius."

I started blushing. "No, not that... it is just a quotation by Lao Tzu that I happen to recall, I'm just a plagiarizer."

"See what I mean? Here's another word I can't even pronounce much less have it in my vocabulary. Who is he anyway?"

"Lao Tzu? He is the father of Taoism. One of the Far East religions... a kind of cult. He is famous for coming up with wise words, I am just copying him."

She really made her observation stick by making it personal, and I loved it. "Know what; you're my Buddha! I do not know Lao and Tao but I know Buddha. I keep a bronze Buddha in my living room. You made it come alive for me. Like Geppetto and Pinocchio."

I cherished the idea that she considered me hers, but I'm not so sure about the Buddha likeness to be all that flattering. I was still enjoying this conversation which is one of our few, with substance. Unfortunately it got interrupted prematurely, when Kathy's husband Paul showed up on crutches. He recently had an Achilles tendon injury which was the reason he was sequestered upstairs in his bedroom. With the help of an orthopedic boot and crutches he was finally moved downstairs to join the party.

He is a tall, boisterous, athletic type you would have a hard time matching with Kathy if you were a contestant at "Who is My Spouse?" The only similarity between them is the angular lines of their noses, jaw bones, and ears.

A group of guests gathered around him as he was helped to a chaise-lounge strategically placed to be visible to all and close enough to the house to minimize his shaky progress on crutches.

"So Mr. Kravchuk, how did you rupture the Achilles?" One of Kathy's prime brownnosers yelled for everyone to hear.

"I was trying to kick his ass in basketball," pointing to Robert, his son.

"Look whose ass is kicked." his son jested right back.

"It's a chip of the old block." brownnoser number two chimed in.

The conversation went on like this before Mr. Kravchuk found himself explaining his recuperation predicament. This was the busiest time at his company that makes poopsicle sticks, match sticks, and toothpicks. With the summer season mostly over, he needs to be out and about for his lively-hood. To boot, his recuperation is long and a real "pain in the butt." And the steroids he has to take for his Psoriasis slows down his healing.

"I'm between a rock and a hard place."

"I know who can cheer you up." Robin exclaimed pointing to me: "My Buddha!"

Now I am really blushing. Good God Robin, you really put me on the spot.

"Who's the Buddha?"

Kravchuk looked around to spot me. "Ok, cheer me up! Come to think of it, you do look like a Buddha."

He accentuated his observation with a chuckle, "Ha! ha! See he already cheered me up."

Robin, having placed me in the worst possible limelight, is visibly uncomfortable. "No, he has these incredible quotations by Lao Tao that really make you think. C'mon Trev roll them out."

I am even more uncomfortable and am desperately looking for an exit from the center of attention, "I can't really think of any right now."

But Robin insisted. and made me blurt out the first thing that occurred to me. "Well, I know a story which is kind of long … which is kind of about ..."

"A story! I can use one now that I am as helpless as a toddler with these crutches and Kathy does everything for me. Kind of everything: I still can eat, piss, crap and sleep, all by myself."

I told them this story I had read in a book about a man, two tigers, a rat, and a strawberry that about plant. I took a long gulp and started "It goes something like this."

"One fine morning, in order to revive his constitution and invigorate his mind, a man decides to take a stroll in the woods. As he is absorbed in his thoughts and the nature that engulfed him, he noticed that he was being followed by a tiger.

The longer I was able to control my insecurities the bolder my narration got.

The predator was at a safe distance for the moment but he was concerned that the coincidence in the direction of movement might be more than just a chance. So, he hastened his pace. To his chagrin, so did the tiger. Little by little his haste grew into panic and he found himself running as fast as he could with the tiger in hot pursuit.

Suddenly he came to a deep precipice. Sensing the eminent danger was becoming more acute every second, he grabbed a vine nearby and started climbing down the side of the cliff. As he was feeling comfortable with his move, he heard the now familiar panting of the tiger getting louder, not fainter. This made him stop and look down. There was another tiger waiting for him at the valley below.

Now that I had just about everyone's full attention. I proceeded with greater confidence:

Despite this double jeopardy, he thought that he could wait at least one of the tigers out, by resting upon a ledge on the side of the cliff. This is when he also noticed that there was a new critter sound in the air: the gnawing of a rat.

His vine was now a sharpening instrument for the incisors of a rat that apparently ruminated on the side of the cliff as well.

At this moment of utter despair, as if slipping into a state of denial, he spotted a juicy ripe strawberry hanging off of a bush on the side of the cliff. It was within his reach. With a broad smile on his face, he lost all sense of danger and plucked the strawberry and tossed it in his mouth, savoring the sweet tart flavor and aroma of the fruit that has been prepared by nature for this singular opportunity for him to enjoy, at this particular hour, on this particular fine day. "

Having listened to the entire thing patiently Mr. Kravchuk said, "What does it mean, Mr. Buddha? Tell us.".

"He is in denial." Someone began to explain. "Denial is the first stage of dealing with catastrophe."

Someone else summarized, "He is screwed, and that's what. He is about to fall into the saliva lubricated jaws of the tiger below, which is first going to train his claws on him, before gnawing on his carotid artery. How does this cheer up anyone?'

A third guest growled, "Get real guys, this is a metaphor for things. The tigers represent life's pains in the butt. Like Mr. Kravchuk here."

An unidentified voice chuckled, "Kathy she is calling your hubby a pain in the butt. Ha ha!"

The first pontificate jumped into the fray again, "No. Listen he is between two things; his healing, and his job. In fact three, the steroids, which could be the rat gnawing at him."

"Who is the strawberry then?"

This is when Mr. K turned to Kathy with a broad gesture of his right arm drawing a large arc in the air as if he is Fred Astaire beckoning Ginger Rogers to the stage.

"That would be my Kat!"

The episode ended with *oh*'s and *ah*'s; turning my humiliating start into a minor triumph the likes of which I had never experienced in a social occasion like this. And I owed it all to Robin. She is the girl for me. I turned and looked at her. When she looked back, I swear her eyes were acknowledging my affection for her.

We left the party later than most. Robin drove me home. During the entire ride, I thought about a reason to invite her in. Needless to say my participation in the conversation was detached. When we finally stopped, it was still early and I could not come up with the equivalent of the nightcap for this time of day.

"Trev, you are a damn shy Buddha, but you were magnificent tonight. I never thought you had it in you."

"Thanks, well you put me up to it. It was your brilliance. But I have a lot more from where that came… including my books…"

"I bet the entire ride you have been trying to come up with a line to try to lure me into your pad."

Am I that transparent? Emboldened by Lao Tzu *When you are content to be simply yourself and don't compare or compete, everybody will respect you.* I fessed up.

"As a matter of fact…"

"Ok I'd love to."

She turned off the engine. Took me by the hand and we went up to my modest apartment. She was in control and I was in seventh heaven. I broke out the wine. She took me into the bedroom and sat me on the bed.

She sat on my lap and we started kissing. Her lips alone were luscious enough to give me an erection. Her ass rubbing against my penis moved matters beyond control. I pulled back.

"I'm going to come."

"Come my sweet I'll help you."

She got off of me and laid me on my back. She took of her top revealing her youthful, Aphrodite breasts. I reached out instinctively and cupped them with eyes closed. She pulled down my pants and slid down. The ecstasy I was drawing from my hands could not be replaced even by the rock hard instrument by my groin.

Kay considered *fellatio* too demeaning to engage, while *Cunnilingus*– both her terms – was fine so long as I liked it, which I did. It made her more receptive to my advances and eased her anxious and technical approach to sex. In Kay's case pain was involved. This clearly contributed to the fact that we have not conceived but one child, which is a momentous accomplishment for a woman who would rather forget about her body below the belt than expand her dopamine needs outside of insulting her spouse. I am able to keep Ed out of my life in daily encounters, but I find it difficult in the lower levels of consciousness, which is where Robin took me as swiftly as a hawk diving for her prey with a graceful swoosh.

This is unmistakably the most exquisite delight of my life physically and emotionally. I was completely lost when something inside me – a remnant form sex with Kay no doubt – said: What about her?

And I spoke. "What about you?" She stopped, looked up with my erect and pulsating penis in front of her lips.

"It's ok; I have my period. I'm managing her too."

Just at the nick of time, she proceeded with her *pièce de résistance* act, sending me off somewhere I had never been before. She came with a groan synchronized with my moans. She timed it perfectly.

The night ended with a shower, dinner at the sushi restaurant down the street, and a peaceful sleep in each other's arms in my humble apartment.

HERMIT CRAB - Sail A'non

HERMIT CRAB - Sail A'non

Twelve
Breakdown

I am head over heels in love and beyond platonic expectations. After 40 years of undiagnosed unhappiness, I started having wet dreams and enjoyable masturbation. We did not find the occasion to be intimate again for days. I could not afford to be too pushy. While she is warm and receptive, it is a very busy week at the Y and our physical intimacy did not go beyond necking. I was not fully confident about her feelings. After all we slept together only once, and that by definition is no assurance that things will necessarily escalate from there on. In the absence of a sage mentor taking us to the more advanced chapters of the *Shades of Gray*, where should we get our sexual training but from the silver screen?

I planned a weekend of delights – movies, food, sex, laughter and yes boundless love. I went to the Y and caught her between engagements to invite her in person. I brought her a box of raw chocolate that she likes. We are on for Friday after work. I used one of Ed's tricks and ordered gourmet dishes from the Japanese restaurant that we both enjoy.

Even though they do not deliver I could not wait for the week to end and left work early to set things up. Unavoidably, this recalls my last supper with Kay and Jay. This is the second bookend to my expected closures – a definite closure on Ed and one that will start Travis on his journey. If that was Good Friday this will be Christmas. That means less to a venerable Jew, but it means a great deal to Trev who is eager to let legacy behind and realize the promise of life.

I decked out my apartment as best as I could, paying particular attention to the dining table and the bedroom. On the dining table, I arranged the new accoutrements I bought during the week just for this occasion. The silverware and the china were coordinated but the napkins and the napkin holders were each of a different theme. On my salary I am able to afford things only on sale.

I had to improvise the table cloth since I had forgotten about it all together. I folded up a new bed sheet to fit the size of my small table. In the candlelight, it will look good enough. I took out all of the serving plates and utensils I could find. I had to borrow a few from one of our neighbors, Mr. and Mrs. Chu, a couple with a young daughter residing in the apartment at the end of the hallway. I always see them strolling in and out of the elevator, and we make eye contact before nodding politely. I remember from the days when Jay was a toddler Kay and I felt empathy for people who pleasantly interacted with him.

I ended up with more serving utensils and dishes than I needed. Out of politeness I did not reject any of the pile of stuff they handed me under the suspicious gaze of the little one. Who knows maybe someday Robin and I too will be; well I'm getting too far ahead of the game.

I placed my Buddha statuette, 14" tall, on the bed stand for luck and as an acknowledgement of the affectionate spin she puts on, when she says "Trev my Buddha"

Robin is late. I need her car to pick up the food. When she finally arrived 45 minutes late, I sensed that she was tense and distant.

"What's wrong?"

"Nothing," she replied. "I guess I'm a little under the weather."

"I'm sorry. We'll fix that right away."

I had spent a good penny on a few bottles of Chateau Saint Michelle. I opened the 2003 Meritage from their Artist Series and I poured two healthy-size wine glasses. She finished her glass in a few minutes. Clearly there was something going on that I should not be so eager to find out.

"May I borrow your car to pick up the food? You know, I am not the best cook in the world, so I decided to hire the chef at Umi."

This seemed to perk her up a bit. I was concerned about the rest of the evening but willing to face whatever was to transpire this evening. I feel confident and ready to overcome all obstacles for my last chance for happiness. When I returned from Umi, in about two-quarter's time, I found my apartment door ajar. Surprised but not alarmed I entered the small vestibule.

"Honey I'm ho-o-me! I brought you sustenance. You'll perk up in no time."

As I turned around and walked towards the dining area, I was stunned. I could not comprehend what lay before my eyes. The table I had set with such care was bare, with the entire setting scattered around the floor. The CD player was smashed along with all of the items that were on the shelf. Three of the four chairs were lying on their sides. My framed O'Keefe posters were also on the floor. There was nothing left in its place, as if a powerful earthquake had hit my flat.

This was such an implausible sight that first I took the implausible explanation provided by the idea of the earthquake to be the case, even though I had not seen a single evidence to suggest it before I entered my apartment. As I was trying to sort things out the thought of Robin flashed through my mind: I was sick with panic. Is she ok? Did she do this? Who did this?

Everything seemed so implausible that I began to doubt my senses. All of these thoughts were flashing through my head at the speed of light. I hit the brakes and backed to an earlier thought. Is Robin ok?

The packages of food I was still holding onto slipped out of my hands and fell on the floor with a thud. I moved to the living room where the furniture was similarly thrashed. I started to panic, and ran into the bedroom. Although the bed was in disarray it was in its place. There were red stains all over it. The first proposal that jumped into my head: Blood!

I wanted to run away. For a second eminent danger and concern for Robin tussled in my gut. When I noticed that the blood stains were leading to the bathroom, I rushed in and found her curled up in the tiny space between the bath tub and the commode on a small puddle of blood. I almost passed out from the sight of blood. Mustering up all of my strength I lunged forward trying to help her up, not thinking if she was conscious or even alive. She pushed me back with a force I did not expect from someone in her condition.

"Get away from me!"

I was stunned. She collapsed back into her tiny space with eyes closed. She was almost catatonic. Did she do this to herself? Denial! The two tigers, the rat, or the strawberry; which one is she? I had to do something. Instinctively, I pulled out my cell and dialed 911.

"Yes there is a severe trauma victim here. The address is…"

I can hardly remember what I said, but once the medics arrived and gave her a sedative shot, she was mobile enough to be carried to the ambulance on a gurney. I followed the ambulance with Robin's car; and waited for hours at the emergency department. She was x-rayed, scanned, treated for cuts bruises and lacerations, all over her body. It is going to be a long night, and not of the kind I had planned. A burning sensation slid down my chest into my gut. What happened? Who did this to her? Why?

"Sir; can you tell us what happened?"

Since there is obvious foul play, the hospital staff has called the police and I am probably the prime suspect. A bigger ball of fire slid from my throat all the way down to my bowels. I almost crapped in my pants. I had an unstoppable urge to piss. I blushed from this triple whammy and called upon Travis, the confident go-get'm-guy to take over.

"I'll tell you what I know."

"I'm Officer Benson, I'm investigating this case. We suspect foul play. Can you come with us to the station?"

"Sure."

No hesitation in my voice despite my flustered face.

"May I go to the bathroom first?"

Officer Benson though for a moment and then escorted me to the bathroom, apparently dismissing the thought that I could ever be a flight risk. After a short ride in a patrol car, I was taken into what I can only assume to be an interrogation room. What did I get myself into?

"What is your relationship to Ms. Carter?"

"I'm her boyfriend." There is no room for answers with too much ambiguity.

"Does she have a next of kin?"

"I don't... oh, yes, she does. She has a brother: Ronald Carter. He lives in Chicago. He is a friend of mine."

"Do you have a number for him?"

"No, I do not, not with me anyway."

This was a fib, but I could easily have misplaced it. I just did not want to exaggerate my relationship with Ronny.

"That's ok; we'll get it from Ms. Carter when she is able to talk to us."

This was my turn to ask, "How is she? I'm very worried about her."

Ignoring my query the cop continued with the interrogation, asking me to explain what happened. Stopping me with questions about my narration of the evening's events: How long was I gone? What was the name of the restaurant and its location? Why didn't I have the food delivered instead of picking it up? Did Robin have enemies? Could I think of anyone who would want to do this to her? Did I notice anything strange in the last few days?

He also informed me that my apartment is now a crime scene and is being processed by detectives as we spoke. After he was done with me, he informed me that they would check my testimony with that of Ms. Carter when she was able. And I should stay put to hear from the police in the next few days.

If I wished I could pick up my things from my apartment and arrange another place to stay for a few days. The detectives may decide to return for further inspection of the "premises." As I drove home, or to whatever was left of it, I began to measure the magnitude of my misfortune.

My "first dinner" night is now officially my nightmare night. I am devastated with Robin's predicament.

I am under suspicion for domestic violence. I am too shaken up to sufficiently regain my composure to return to normal life and work. I am setback all the way to where I was when I stepped out of the plane from Chicago, nearly three months ago with $730 in my pocket.

When I reached the apartment, there was a uniformed cop at the door to escort me. I gathered all that I could pack into my suitcase, when I had walked out of my home on 714 Gist Avenue. When I left, the cop put the crime scene tape back on the door. I walked downstairs and by force of habit checked my mailbox. Much to my surprise I found an envelope with "To My Lovable Buddha" inscribed on it. My heart leapt into my throat. I slipped it into my pocket, casually. The officer either did not notice or did not care. I told him I was heading to the City Hostel. I took a cab to my old stomping ground. After checking in, I went straight up to my room.

There is another resident registered for the room but he is not around. It is passed midnight but this being a Friday night, the Hostel feels empty. I curled up on my bed and opened the envelope with shaking hands and an unbearable sense of apprehension:

"To My Affectionate Buddha: [This already sounds ominous.]

"I am writing because I do not have the courage to face you with the truth. After this night I will not have to explain it in words. You will know. It is better that way. Yet, I am not sure if we will have a chance to talk about things calmly. Therefore, I have to try to put in some words what I know will never fully explain things.

I am not this way because of choice. I was born this way. I have lived with my inner battle almost my entire life. Since I was eight I was like Ronny for many years. Then I decided that I was not being true to myself. I appeared as one thing but knew that I was something else. I had to change. Not change. I had to be what I really am. Is there a word for that, my Buddha?

When I met you I was drawn to you because you are genuine. I was hopeful that you would accept me as I am. Your eyes told me that you are kind and honest. But when I finally worked up the courage to tell Ronny that I was about to steal his boyfriend, I realized that I had no chance with you.

I continue to deceive myself. I have grown so fond of you that I am willing to risk everything. I will try to make it right and natural for us.

If you are willing to accept me as I am, I will be the happiest girl and you would not be reading this. If you are reading this, please know that Lao Tzu said – I looked it up especially for us – "When I let go of what I am, I become what I might be."

*With love,
Robin.*

HERMIT CRAB - Sail A'non

Thirteen
Tumult

My mind goes blank, perhaps for the first time in my life. I collapse on the bed and pass out from stress and exhaustion. When I woke up I was a mess; still wearing the same clothes as the day before. I did not have the energy to take a shower or to think about the events of yesterday.

I staggered out of my room. Stopped at the bagel place where I used to eat during my early days here. It was closed. It is too early for life to begin in Seattle. I kept walking around to pass the time. As the sights and sounds of downtown began to return so did my humanly senses. In turn, they ignited my brain with a twitch and sputter.

How did I get myself into this?

Robin thinks that I am the genuine article. Hah! I am anything but. If she only knew who I really am: certified, self-declared fraud, cheat, and impostor. I don't even know who **I** am. Really, who am I, Travis or Edward? I disgust myself, either way. Travis hated Edward and Edward is just beginning to develop a deep disappointment in Travis and what he has done to Ed.

My dual personality is front and center now. My attempt to change from one thing to another has made me both or neither. At least Robin knows what she is, or what she wants to be. She is no longer a man. She is sensuous, fun, and full of life. What else could I want in a woman? What else could anyone?

I wondered into a Denny's and ordered one of their 6.99 breakfast specials. My diet and workout regime can go to hell. What for? I have ruined at least three lives; Robin's, mine, and the other mine; not to mention all those people I left behind in Baltimore, at least those who cared about me; Jay for sure.

I have the two tigers and the rat on my back, growling and gnawing at me relentlessly. I need my strawberry. I hailed a cab. I arrived at the hospital in 10 minutes. It is not time for visitation yet. I have to wait for another half-hour before I can go in to see her.

"Hey stranger, didn't I tell you she is exceptional."

It is Ronny. When he saw me, his eyes lit up. Since I was still unsure about how I would reconnect with Robin after all that transpired, I was elated to see him as well.

"When did you get here?"

"Just an hour ago."

The police must have contacted him. When we entered Robin's room I saw that she was bandaged top-to-toe with metal braces securing her jaw and a cast on her left wrist. Her eyes were closed. I approached her and held her hand. Her eyes parted for a second. Her lips quivered but there was no smile or sound. She must be in pain or is heavily sedated.

Ronny pointed to the door, "she needs to rest, let's get out."

"Sure?" I said. "Did they tell you how this happened?"

"You mean you don't know?"

"Not a clue."

He was partially serious when he said, "I knew I should not have trusted my sister to a straight guy, but it is what it is."

He continued, "the police learned from the neighbors and other witnesses that two thugs went into your apartment and worked her over and left before you arrived."

"Why? Is this a hate crime or something?"

Ronny rolled his eyes. "Trevor; where you at my friend? This is Seattle, not the *Deliverance* domain."

I was still trying to understand, "mean… why would they ever do this to her? Was she in trouble or something?"

"One of the cops said that they were asking about you."

"Me? Who are these people?"

How many ways can things go wrong?

"They have no clue. The cops were planning to see you today; to see if you can help."

"Crap!" Ed took over the conversation, "I bet Kay has something to do with this."

"Who is this Kay? Your ex?"

"I don't have an ex."

He looked at me with suspicion.

"I've had it with these cops. They interrogated me for close to an hour yesterday. I am a mess. Look at me. I couldn't get into my apartment; couldn't take a shower."

"I can tell."

Ignoring Ronny's sarcasm I elaborated, "have to get myself together, before I can take more of this stuff."

My pulse was beginning to race trying to catch up with the rest of me. If this is Kay, I am screwed. What if it is Kay? I have a good mind to go to the police and put them on her for trying to hurt, even kill me. But there is a price to pay, a price too dear, considering all that I have gone through for the past several years. I would have to reveal my identity. Furthermore, I would have to risk prosecution for all the fraud and illegal shenanigans I carried out.

This would be worse than Kay's wrath. I need to calm down and figure things out.

"Ronny, it was good seeing you again. Tell Robin I'll be back [I am not really sure about this]; and I care about her a lot [I am sure about this, and so is Ronny]"

"Be cool and do not skip town, now. Seattle police will have your ass for it." He winked and gave me a hug.

His touch reminded me of Robin's caress. Ronny also knows who he is and what he is up to. He is comfortable in his own skin. I'm the only one it seems who is going nowhere with his new *shell*.

I left the hospital and took a cab. There is no time to waste. I have to skip town until things quiet down. But what about the police, they told me to stay put. Nice going Trev, Ed, whoever the fuck you are. Now you are about to be a fugitive, one way or another! And let me tell you; you are no Buddha! You are not cool, or even halfway sane. At best, you are Sisyphus, each time you roll the boulder up the hill a little, it rolls right back crashing on top of you.

I have to hide away for a little at least until the eye of the storm blows over. I decided to go home and clear out everything that has Trev's insignia; just in case I can still hide in his skin.

There were no cops at the door. The crime scene tape was gone. As far as the condo administration is concerned, this is probably just a domestic disturbance, which would mean that I may have to move out of here. I had my personals at the hostel, all I needed were the vital documents and anything of value, until it was safe to come back and pick up the furniture.

The apartment stunk of rotting fish. The furniture was in the same disarray as it was before. I went to work straightening things up, dumping broken plates, old magazines, and the spoiled sushi still in its packaging, into the trash bin. The bed sheet which was stained with Robin's blood was gone. I suppose it is with the police as evidence. I had used it to wipe Robin's blood off of the bathroom floor. So at best, it is contaminated evidence. I'll let the cops worry about that.

Once the apartment looked tidy enough I started sorting out the papers I had in a file box which was unceremoniously dumped inside the bedroom closet where I kept them. I placed all papers that had to do with bank, credit card, and utility transactions in my backpack that I had purchased for Yoga sessions at the Y.

Irony; how could things go so wrong, and so soon? Damn you Kay, will I never get rid of you? The though woke up my drive to get away and wipe her out of Trev's life as well. I did it once, I can do it again. I will learn from this and do it absolutely right the next time. I bet someone discovered the mail I received at the bureau under pseudo names; or checked the records at the Hostel International. This is no *Law and Order* but Kay is no ordinary wicked chick, either.

    I decided to take my copies of Joyce and *Moby Dick* that have been with me literally my entire life. I found my birth certificate and all official correspondence about the driver's license and leases. Come to think of it, if they were indeed working for Kay, why didn't the goons take any of this stuff? I assume they were here to kidnap me, to teach me a lesson, or something like that; not to conduct an inquiry. None of this makes any sense but I will figure things out once I get myself tucked safely into my hermit crab shell once again. In any case, they blew it. I was lucky to be absent; while my poor Robin got the working over on my behalf.

    I picked up the Buddha statuette and stuffed it into the backpack as well. I had some cash stashed into its hollow center just for emergencies. I walked into the living room. One last glance; it looks almost normal.

    As I made my way to the door, I heard clicking sounds from the hallway right outside of the door. I froze. Someone is shimmying the lock. Is it the police? Shit, should I even be here? Why would the police shimmy the lock like a burglar.

"Who is there?"

Fuck, what if these are the goons on a return visit? Ronny thought they were really after me and probably are hell bent on working me over probably a lot more than they did Robin. Compose yourself Trev! Where can I hide? Forget that. How can I get away? The noises from the outside are intensifying. Now I can hear inaudible conversation. These are male voices.

I ran to the kitchen with my backpack hanging off of my shoulder. I opened the window leading to the metal-grate fire stairs as quietly as I could. I pushed my body through the narrow opening of the double hung and lowered it down behind me. Just as the last sound wave squeezed through the ever narrowing opening of the window, I heard my door open.

I shuffled down the stairs with rapid clown like motions. The steps are narrow and I am using the heels of my boots for traction with the toes spread wide open. I slipped on a few steps jamming my calf muscle against the metal edge of the tread. I do not have the luxury to let the pain turn into a yelp for fear of revealing my location, let alone stop and see if I'm bleeding. I reached the sloped lawn at the back of the condo. There is still no sign that anyone is after me.

I began to walk then slide on my ass, down the hillside. I do not dare go to the front of the building where I would surely be spotted right away. My faux-alligator boots are not the best for traction on the grassy slope. I reverted to my clown-like motions, spreading my legs apart without losing balance. The Buddha statuette is banging against my back with each downward glide. It is the heaviest item I am carrying, but this is no time to bailout payload.

The backpack strap around my right shoulder and my leather jacket collar are pressing uncomfortably against my double chin. Constricted by the pull of the hillside against my jeans, I am getting a serious wedgie. My belt is cutting into my triple belly flab. I am flustered and out of breadth. Somehow there is a connection here to Sisyphus. Instead of his payload coming down on him, he is the one going down like the boulder. Metaphorically speaking, we are two peas in a pod.

The hillside got steeper towards the end. My hands have cuts and my ass is hurting from catching small rocks, bushes and urban debris, some of which is in freefall towards the retaining wall along the sidewalk below. My hemorrhoids are in painful disarray. Out of nowhere I hear this bellowing voice from above:

"There he is!"

I strain to look up and someone is looking out of the window on the fire-stair of my condo. Panic is my self-indulgent friend. I can hardly keep it at bay. My legs are shaking from exertion and the adrenalin jolt. I slip and roll on my side all the way to the retaining wall only to stop at a sturdy bush. I must look totally ridiculous lying on a bush by a retaining wall, my legs in pretzel formation, and my backpack unceremoniously landing on my face with the momentum of my slide. The Buddha must have hit my right cheek and it is aching like hell. I have no time for self-pity.

I pick myself up quickly and jump over the wall onto the sidewalk, ending up just a few feet from a young girl walking along the sidewalk. She jumps up like a frog and screams bloody hell. I hastily apologize and start in the opposite direction, tugging my jacket up and wedgie down as best as I can. My jeans are torn in the left leg, its seat is covered with mud, and snot is running down my nostrils. I wipe it with my left sleeve. Leather against snot is not very effective.

I cross the road paying as little attention to the traffic as I can. There is not a taxi in sight. Finally, I have my backpack secured on both shoulders. I'm trying to look as normal as possible under the circumstances. My left shoulder is aching badly. I try to hail a taxi with the right arm raised, New York style.

Finally, a car slows down. It is not a marked taxi. It looks like a private moonlight. Beggars can't be choosers. As it stops in front of me, I realize that this is no taxi it's a Russian made limo known as ZIL *(or Zavod Imeni Likhachova),* around here. The guy in the passenger seat jumps out and grabs me. He shoves me towards the back seat before I can make a move. This is a WWF wrestler type, short, broad, agile, and with Vise-Grip hands. I open my mouth to scream for help just as the brut bangs my head against the rear door frame while trying to shove me inside. What comes out of my mouth is more of an unintelligible scream of pain than an appeal for help.

I do not know if anyone heard me or saw my kidnapping, but I heard the wrestler-type loud and clear as he sat beside me and slammed the door shut. He informed me that if I ever plan to make any more sounds like that, he would be inclined to make fish food out of me for the fish market, which incidentally is to the right as we drive past. The goon at the driver's seat, who is younger, smaller, well-trimmed and tailored, mob type, says.

"Let's wait for Elian."

The wrestler guy responds, "he is busy wiping this shithead's pad clean. If we don't hook up now, he'll know where to find us. And how many times did I tell you no names you knuckle head. Shut up and drive."

We start moving without haste. These guys are the real deal operating with impunity in broad daylight. I am in serious trouble. The exhaustion and the fear turned me into a pile of dough plastered all over the backseat. Even if I wanted to resist and scream, I neither have the energy nor the guts to do either. I attempt to wipe my nose again, this time with my shirt sleeve. My nose is bleeding, probably from the bang on my head or the terror of it all. These guys would not think twice about wasting me.

"This douche bag is falling apart; are you sure we got the right guy here?"

The slick looking driver replies. "Eli thinks so. He is a goddamn snitch, what the hell do you expect?"

"I said no names, wise guy. Why are you do'in it again?"

"No matter, the cat is out of the bag anyhow."

"Stop thinking so much and drive! You're gon'na hurt your brain. This guy is wasted beyond belief."

I am sure now that Kay bought a contract on me? How can she sink so low? My wife of 16 years and I didn't know the kind of person she is and what she is capable of. It must have been inside her, hidden behind all the *flim-flam-flirt* she dished out at strategic moments. I can't believe she can be so evil. No wonder I saw her as the devil incarnate in my Cape May nightmare.

"I'll pay you more!" I screamed. "Don't kill me man, I'm not worth it."

They both started laughing.

"He is a nutcase," announced Slick.

"He is scared shitless." replied the Wrestler.

"I have money! Pleeeease." I begged.

"He has money you hear? The old man wants to bribe us. What do you say? Shall we take his money too?"

He was poking me in the belly, in the groin, on the side with his stubby fingers, each time making me jump and moan with pain that seemed to emanate from all over.

After a short ride we arrived at a small, warehouse-looking building at the back of the wharf. There was no Eli or anyone else for that matter. They have to pry me lose from the seat, into which I had melted like wax in a mold. I am not resisting but my flesh, fat and bones are glued to the upholstery through invisible bonds of gravity.

Finally, the two of them drag me out; carry me into the warehouse; and drop me on the concrete floor as if depositing a sack of garbage into the dumpster. Slick lights a cigarette taking a deep breath as if the smoke was filling him up with magical, restorative powers.

"This creep is heavy, man!"

He kicks me on the side voiding my lungs that are in great distress to start out with. I mean nothing to them. When I am able to breathe again, I inhale like a vacuum cleaner on steroids. The pain is unbearable. Do they have to torture me? As I exhale with the same intensity I scream.

"Get it over with you bastards, enough is enough!"

Wrestler is surprised by my new found energy, "hey look at him, he's got spunk. He may well be our guy, after all."

"Where's Eli? When are we going to start?" Slick responds.

Wrestler is eager to get down to business, "what's your name you fuck face? Who are you?"

The blood on my face is now being diluted by tears. I am not sure of the right answer. Who are they looking for; Ed or Travis?

"Travis. I'm Travis." I yelled.

"Would that be Travis Titus, now, you fat faggot? When did you gain all this blubber?" Wrestler asks. "Is he supposed to look like this?"

"We'll wait for Eli, he'll know."

I decided to change tacks and see if the truth would help.

"Ok you got me damn it! Ok! I'm not Travis, I am Edward, Edward Amado; I swear I am not Travis."

I could hardly finish my sentence. Slick went ballistic. He was on me like an enraged bull, kicking and punching me with reckless abandon. "Stop lying you shit-bag! Who the hell are you? Tell me the truth! Who's this Edward shit? Is he one of your snitch buddies?"

He pulls a switchblade; turns me over; pulls apart the front of my button down shirt and proceeds to cut the front of my T-shirt open. Sitting on top of me, he grabs my left nipple. My arms instinctively flex and I swing them towards him; but not before the motion thrusts the sharp blade across my chest and I feel this instant pain flashing down through my left side. Blood is running down my chest.

The jolt of my body and my flailing arms are enough to knock Slick off of me. He was not prepared for such a violent spasm from a jellyfish that was lying helplessly on the floor, just a second earlier. He loses it. He is kicking me with all his might. From exposure to continuous pain and my over-acting adrenal gland my body has become numb.

"You fucking faggot, you lying ho. I'm gon'na make you my bitch you hear. I'm gon'na fuck your ass!"

Wrestler tries to step in, "cool it, cool it, man! Before you waste this guy we got'ta be sure. The other day, we fucked up with that girl, weirdo shit woman, and heard it from Sergei."

Slick snaps at him, "I thought there were no names man!"

"You cool it first, no repeats of yesterday's fuckup!"

With that the wrestler type grabs me by the collar, or what was left of it, and props me up; leans into my ear and whispers. "Who are you? Tell us the truth and live."

I am completely exasperated by now, "Who do you want me to be? Tell me! I'll be that!"

He throws me down, face first. I land on my cheek that is already covered with blood, saliva and tears. He kicks me in the ass. "This guy is a clown. He is either too smart or too dumb."

Now Slick is back. I felt a tug on the back of my belt and it snapped open. He is using his blade again. He cuts open the back of my pants.

"Now I'll learn you about how it feels to be my bitch. This is the training you missed when you became a snitch."

My ass smeared with crap throws him back for a moment, "Phew, he's shit in his pants; you asshole!"

I feel the pressure of a solid object between my buttocks.

"How does that feel huh?' How does it feel to be fucked by a piece, huh? Is that too much for you, you god damn bastard?"

I spring up to my feet like a released spring. I start to run but trip on my pants that are still wrapped around my knees. I stumble, but keep my balance. With both fists clenched, swollen left eye, bloodied and torn shirt, boots and leather jacket still on, I scream.

"Cut it out!"

My voice is muffled and weak. It certainly did not improve my miserable state. If anything it amplified my pathos. I yell again with greater effect.

"Cut. It. Out!"

Rage is swelling up inside. "I am Edward Amado, you morons. I am an impostor. I'm not Trev. Why don't you get your damn facts right? Am I supposed to do your research for you? What kind of incompetent hitman are you?"

At first, with this unexpected display of energy and assertiveness, both Slick and Wrestler are startled enough to just watch with amusement and genuine interest to see what the heck I was up to. But my last statement must have really ticked off Wrestler. He pulls out his piece from the holster inside his jacket and proceeds to screw on what looks like a silencer.

I am stunned. It is like watching a movie. They are really going to whack me. I must have convinced them that I am really Ed; and after all, this must be Kay's doing. I turn around and try to run once more, this time towards the warehouse doors, forgetting that my pants are still in the way, wrapped around my ankles. As I fall, I see a tall, lanky silhouette against the light from the warehouse doors.

"What the hell are you boys up to? This is supposed to be a clean hit not a piñata party."

He has a Hispanic accent, unlike these two who are definitely East European. He must be Elian, the one they've been waiting for,.

Wrestler, "hey man, where have you been?'

Slick, "we were having a little fun."

I was still lying on the floor on my belly. They turn me over.

Eli leans over and looks at my face closely, "how'm I supposed to ID him? Look at his face. I can't even see it. Clean this crap off of his face. Do you have some beer or something in the car? Wash his damn face."

Slick, "You wash it."

Eli, "Look, I came all the way from Boston to ID this creep. You goons were supposed to grab him not fuck him over like this."

Wrestler, "Who're you calling a goon?"

Eli, "Stop the crap. Let's be professional like; ok?"

Slick, "I'm not wasting my Belgian beer on this looser."

With these words Slick came over and unzipped his pants and a second later I felt this warm stream of piss splatter all over my face. I rolled over as fast as I could but his aim was accurate and followed me around.

"You are disgusting!" After all, Eli seems to be the most civilized goon in the bunch.

Wrestler also seems outraged, "what the fuck are you doing, you pervert? Are you getting off on this looser? You damn flasher."

"Shut up, you guys wanted clean, I cleaned him up for you. If you don't like it, bring your own damn beer to the pissing party. Ha, ha!"

Drenched in piss, I am suffocating with nausea. Ammonia and whatever else this monster had go through his kidneys is busting my lungs. Stuff is burning into the cuts on my face and my eyes. I feel a grip on my hair. It is Eli. He lifts my head and turns my face towards him.

"He is not Titsy."

Now I know what my middle name is supposed to be.

Wrestler is all business now, "are you sure?"

"Sure I'm sure. You think I'm gon'na blow this one?"

Wrestler, "so what are we going to do with this motherfucker?"

"Let's waste him." jumps in Slick.

"Look, you guys already screwed up big time with the dame. We don't even know who this loser is. No more publicity." Eli speaks with authority.

"She was no dame. She was a pervert."

They are talking about Robin.

"No matter, let's clear out of here; back to square one."

My arms are free. I try to wipe my face off. Leather on piss is just as ineffective as it is on snot. I still have the smell of urine in my nose and mouth. My eyes are hardly functioning. There is piss even in my ears. Someone grips my collar again. It is the Wrestler. He whispers in my ear.

"You dun'no how lucky you are."

I open my mouth to say something but the only thing that comes out is half digested humus, pita bread, and Russian salad. It lands in front of him splattering his shoes and pants with small dots of white and pink particles. He slams my face against the floor.

"You slime bag, you fuck face, you goddamn faggot!"

I heard an explosion and felt an unbearable pain in my left knee.

"What the hell did you do that for?"

"He puked on me. What am I supposed to do?"

As they walk away seemingly oblivious to my predicament, the last thing I heard before I pass out is:

"Ok I'll call 911."

HERMIT CRAB - Sail A'non

Fourteen
Redemption

Shalom!

I am in a large room with four walls and a high ceiling. It's dark. There are no lamps. As my eyes adjust to the uneven light modulated by rays of sunlight penetrating from around the corners of the shades and a crack in the dark walnut paneling, I discriminate seats arranged against the walls like so many soldiers. Each one is occupied. All are silently still.

Dad: *Edward, why did you do it my boy*
Mom: *He was bored; should teach him a lesson marrying a shiksa.*
Jay: *Dad, why did you do it?*
Saeed: *Because he could. He is the Brainiac*
Kay: *Tsk, tsk.*
Travis: *Ed, why did you do it?*
Ed: *You tell me.*
Dad: *Okay you were bored. Why did you run away? Where is your chutzpah?*
Mom: *He left it at his bar mitzvah. I had been changing him twice a day since he was a baby.*

Robin: *He lacked love; he deserved it. Is that a sin?*

Zoltan: *There is no sin if you are true to yourself.*

Ronny: *Amen!*

Jake: *Cick-gaak, cick-gaak!*

Rabbi: *"Judaism teaches that sin is an act, and not a state of being. Humankind was not created with an inclination to do evil, but has that inclination 'from his youth' Genesis 8:21."*

Cop: *He is almost 56. He is no spring chicken.*

Travis: *Ed, why did you involve me? I am a snitch. I am in the witness protection program. I cannot be in two places at once. You moron!*

Robin: *It's his life, not yours. Tsk, tsk, tsk. He has free will, id, ego, and all of that. He has Buddha, Freud, Mohammed, Moses in his blood, for Christ's sake!*

Zoltan: *Give me a break. You left out Zarathustra. Who gave you the right to give him the third degree?*

Cop: *I can do that if I want to.*

Robin: *Life is a journey, not a state of being. Change is inevitable. This or that, it is based on choice. It's none of your business, even if I want to be a man, a woman or neither. What is it to you if he wants to be Edward or Travis? Who is he hurting? Kay is happy without the worm. I'm happy with the puppy. Hunky dory!*

Cop: The mob is pissed. They got the wrong guy.
Zoltan: Pig!
Dad: Are you happy son?
Jay: Are you happy Dad?
Jake: Cick-gaak, cick-gaak! I'm happy.
Travis: It hurts.
Dad/Jay: Who asked you?
Robin: You did.
Dad/Jay: Who asked you?
Saeed: Rabin and Arafat.
Dad: Oy vey!
Jay: Rat tat tat!
Mom: Shh! keep quiet when grownups are talking.
Robin: Fuck yourself old woman! This is what ruins everyone's life. How will you get anywhere if you are not willing to try? Do we have to sit at these chairs for the rest of the day? Fuck this getup. Someone help me change it.
Obi: I will.

All: *Yes we can?*
Ed: *I did not do it. He did it.*
Travis: *Blame it on your alter ego, go ahead! If it weren't for me you'd still be licking her ass, caressing your stupid books in a stupid basement, and masturbating in the kitchen. I took you places!*
Ed: *You got me into this mess. Look at the scars, bandages, crutches, casts, and shit I have on. Besides, I made you. You are not accountable.*
Travis: *You discovered me. I was there the entire time. Besides, everyone wears scars, bandages, crutches, casts, and shit. Don't brag.*
Dad: *No, no you weren't there. Kay put you there. She is a shiksa.*
Jake: *Shiksa, shiksa, shiksa!*
All: *Shut up old man!!*
Ed: *Why did I discover you? Why so late? Why did I bring you out? I am no Jekyll.*
Travis: *But I'm Hide. Hide and seek. Cop-hide and mob-seek.*
Ed: *Now I get it. I'm so sorry, sob, sob, sob…*
Robin: *What's done is done. I'm tired of this crap. I am witness for the prosecution and I declare this session closed!*

With these words, Robin got up and started to draw the shades open and to rip out the paneling. The chairs disappeared into cavities of brown light one by one, along with their occupants. Only Jay, Jake, and Robin are left behind. The room is glowing with light. The floor is covered with a brown haze. As Robin approaches me like Cinderella descending so many steps in a ballroom, her long dress skirt sucks up the brown haze. She brings her face close to mine. She reaches over the top of her head with one hand and pulls away her face mask revealing Kay's angelic face. We kiss passionately as Jake flaps his wings.

I wake up from my recurring dream. It is late afternoon. My copies of Joyce and *Moby Dick* are resting on my bedside with my wireframe glasses on top. I am lying in bed with my knee in a cast, bandages on my left arm, stitches on my face and head, and an IV sticking out of my right arm. Despite the physical damages, I feel peaceful.

Through the door, I can see a sliver of Jay's image. He is in his room, at the far end of the hallway, reading on his bed. It must be Sunday. There is some tranquility in the air that you only get after you either complete or give up on the ambitions of the weekend and resign to the laggard progression of time.

I can also see Kay in the near room, probably working on her next jamming project. She usually drives out to a nearby organic produce farm to buy up a lot of good stuff. We are the beneficiaries of her passion for preserves and jams, the equal of which you will not find in local markets. She makes them with care; serves them with love. Her figure is elegant, hair flowing over her shoulders, arms resting gently on her desk. Every now and then she tosses her hair to the left like a butterfly's wing navigating through a gentle breeze. I should be certified for even thinking of her as ugly or evil.

She has been utterly magnanimous in taking me back and trying to nurse me to health. After discovering my disappearance, she has become genuinely worried. She consulted friends and family, alerted the police, but most certainly did not send those goons after me. How could I even imagine that? She put ads in the *Baltimore Sun* and entered my profile in the *NamUs* database – talk about a perfect irony.

After she found out about Robin and I from police reports, we had a serious heart to heart talk. I did not detect resentment, anger or hatred in her demeanor. Nor was she sarcastic and disparaging upon discovering that Robin is transgender. She was disappointed and jealous; but she took me back. She forgave me. I was trying too hard to covet what I had not, instead of embracing what was in front of me. She is my wife, partner, and, yes, love of my life.

Jay has changed in the span of the few months that I was gone. He doesn't seem to be as close to me as we were the night before I left. He appears to be more his own person; seeks less of my company or advice. He is definitely closer to Kay. They have bonded more than I could ever imagine. He helps with her jamming and she usually provides the sage advice when he needs it.

When it comes to me, I am not confused anymore about who am I or what I want to be. When I was Travis, and that I can say with some confidence of its truthfulness, I found fulfillment in deciding for myself, which I considered to be the equivalent of emancipation from externals, notably the institutions of life, marriage, family relations, religion and societal expectations.

I learned from Jay, who did the research from police reports and conversations with medical and law enforcement people; he came to the conclusion that the id of Travis Titus, my empty shell, was vacated months before by a mob informant with that name and assumed a completely different identity. He was recruited into the witness protection program and had disappeared into the woodwork.

I as Travis happened to emerge into the scene shortly after, while the Boston Irish mob, betrayed by ole' Travis, was still looking for him. By stepping into his shell I became the new occupant of his former identity and the target for the mob.

Jay also discovered that the mob's pay-or-I'll-break-your-leg operation also had a legitimate collection business that picked up on the plethora of credit card applications I had been filling from Seattle under Travis' name. So, the Irish mob, bought a contract on Travis (now I) with the Russian mob operating out of Seattle. Eli, the ID man, plus Slick, and Wrestler tracked me down but they did not find me in their first try and opted to work Robin over to get to me.

Discovering that she was not a real she, they proceeded to sodomize her. Once they got a hold of me, however, they took their entire frustration on me; turning me into a pulp. On that fateful day, while my body gave out, in Dr. Seuss' famous words, my heart grew a few sizes bigger. Going through the sheer terror and pain of my encounter in the abandoned warehouse at the Seattle wharf made me a better man.

I am not fearful any more. As I look at my Buddha statuette on the mantle of our bedroom fireplace, I can't help but think of Zoltan, Robin and their evocations of Lao Tzu.

"When I let go of what I am, I become what I might be."

Meet Leuqes envisioning the 2018 sequel to **Hermit Crab**

HERMIT CRAB - Sail A'non

www.ingramcontent.com/pod-product-compliance
Lightning Source LLC
Chambersburg PA
CBHW070547050426

42450CB00011B/2757